UPSTREAM

Matt Ehresman

"In this world where everyone seems to be fighting over the limited opportunities for fortune and fame, Matt shows us an untouched paradise available to us all. The problem is, it requires counter-intuitive—rather counter-cultural—thinking. I wish every Christian could embrace the truths Matt shares in this quick read, because then we would start looking more like Christ and less like members of a rat race."

Jonathan Malm
Creative entrepreneur and author of *Created for More*

"At the heart of *Upstream* is a vital question: What does it look like to follow Jesus in 21st-century America? But to answer such a question requires careful reading of both contemporary culture and the heart of God. I'm grateful for people like Matt Ehresman who demonstrate a clear commitment to writing about and living out this good pursuit."

Scott McClellan
Communications pastor and author of *Tell Me a Story*

UPSTREAM

NOTE FROM THE AUTHOR

I love reading.

Actually, let me re-phrase that. Sometimes I *hate* reading.

Lately it seems like a lot of the books I've read and most that I've seen advertised have the same problem; these books have one really great, ground-breaking idea. It's inspiring, encouraging, and funny... for about 30 pages. A chapter or two is really good, and then the author repeats himself for 250 more pages.

Or another thing: A lot of books—and sadly, a lot of "Christian books"—make everything too simple. They use flowery language and cute little inspirational phrases that makes it sound like my problems are silly and easy to fix. A little too... K-Love-y, if you know what I mean.

I hate those books.

In fact, let's not even call them books. Books are too good for us to do that to them. Kind of like "Canadian bacon." Can we get real right here at the beginning? Canadian bacon is not bacon. You're not kidding anyone, Canada.

I hope you'll find this collection of words to be inspiring and interesting and real. I also hope you'll find very little—if any—"fluff" and lots of meat. Probably bacon (and none of the Canadian variety). I wasn't trying to reach a certain word count when I started writing. You'll notice that there are eight chapters here. Eight. A lot of people probably would have pushed themselves to get to ten. A nice, neat multiple of five would have felt a little cleaner. And (spoiler alert) the eight chapters don't even combine to create a fun little acronym at the end. I think they teach you to do that in book-writing school.

Here's the thing; I tried writing more chapters, but they ended up being about things I wasn't passionate about. There may have been a couple good ideas hidden in there somewhere, but I don't want to put you, dear reader, through mediocrity. Instead, I stuck with just the stuff I really cared about, which is apparently eight things.

It probably won't take you long to read this, and that's great. We all love achieving things. You should write "Read Matt's book" on your to-do list, because then you'll feel great after reading this book even if you didn't like it. Seriously—go do that. And maybe cook a quick batch of bacon to enhance your reading experience.

I've read that humans generally make a decision about whether they like someone or not in seven seconds. It probably took you longer than that to read this so far, so if you're still reading, hey—I like you, too. Whether you agree with everything I say in these pages or not, I hope it challenges you to think about what is important and how you can live a better life. So with that, let's get started.

INTRODUCTION

At some point in your life, you probably realized that the "right thing" that you're supposed to do is a lot harder and not as fun as what you really want to do. Homework is not as fun as XBox. You've probably never confused salad for cookie dough. Going for a run outside is better than watching Netflix for so long that your TV actually stops to ask if you're still watching. With each of these dilemmas, you have to make a choice of whether you'll choose to do the hard, right thing or the fun, wrong thing.

For example, have you noticed the war the world is raging on gluten? Apparently gluten is the root cause of every health problem. Stop eating bread and start rubbing essential oils everywhere and you might just be the next Marvel superhero. As true as that may or may not be, I refuse to stop eating bread, even if that is the "right thing" to do.

Although our world looks drastically different today

than it did 2,000 years ago, Jesus had a lot to say about how we should live our lives. And frankly, Jesus said some pretty crazy things.

In one of His most famous teachings, Jesus started with several rules that most of us—regardless of religion, culture, or location—would probably agree are pretty good life principles. In Matthew 5, He taught us not to murder, not to commit adultery, and basically just to be nice to people. Pretty solid advice, but nothing particularly groundbreaking.

But then, Jesus significantly raises the stakes to a level that seems impossible:

> "You have heard that our ancestors were told, 'You must not murder… But I say, if you are even *angry* with someone, you are subject to judgment!" (Matthew 5:21-22)

> "You have heard the commandment that says, 'You must not commit adultery.' But I say, anyone who even *looks at a woman with lust* has already committed adultery with her in his heart." (Matthew 5:27-28)

> "You have heard the law that says, 'Love your neighbor' and hate your enemy. But I say, *love your enemies!* Pray for those who persecute you!" (Matthew 5:43-44)

I wish I could have seen the crowd and the look on the disciples' faces when He said these things. I'm imagining a lot of cricket chirps. If you're a new leader trying to gain large numbers of new followers, this sure is an interesting marketing strategy. Love? Our enemies? Are you sure, Jesus? Shouldn't we be saying "Yes we can!" or something a little more inspiring?

Now, instead of just avoiding a few specific "big" sins, Jesus challenged us to live with much more intentionality. Six times in that chapter, He says something along the lines of "You have heard it said [this obvious sin is bad] *but* [I'm telling you things are different now]." Doing the right thing required doing what no one else wanted to do.

Wide and Narrow

A couple chapters later in Matthew, Jesus uses another interesting analogy:

> "Wide is the gate and broad is the road that leads to destruction, and many enter through it. But small is the gate and narrow the road that leads to life, and only a few find it."
> (Matthew 7:13-14)

Because life is hard, we are generally drawn to simplicity when it is available. If you're on a road trip and Siri gives you two routes to an unfamiliar city, you're going to take the easier one. No brainer. Sure, maybe there are a few unpaved country roads that may shave off a few minutes from your overall travel time, but I'd much rather hop on a freeway and set my cruise control. In this passage, Jesus says something counter-intuitive and instructs us to take a different route—the one *less* traveled.

Jesus says taking this narrow road will lead to life. If you're reading these words, I'm going to go out on a limb and assume you are, indeed, breathing. You have life. So why in the world would we take this smaller road—the harder one full of rocks and thorns—when an easier route is available?

Later in the book of John, Jesus said, "I have come that they may have life, and have it to the *full*" (John 10:10). That word "full" is translated from the original Greek word "perissos," which also translates to strong English words like *vehemently*. Jesus came to give us life that was passionate and zealous and intense. That Greek word can also mean "all around," meaning Jesus came so that *every* aspect of our life would be better and exceed normal expectations. Our lives can be better and more influential than we ever imagined.

This passionate life sounds desirable, but it's rare. Jesus said that only a few people find this life. There's a compelling mystery about that, isn't there? I'm not necessarily the stereotypical Bear Grylls adventurous type, but I do like the idea of finding a secret way to live that is better than the alternative. That desire is what basically every book and article is about these days, isn't it? Jesus says there is a best way to live, but only a few people will choose to do so. Doesn't that grab your attention? Don't you get the feeling that the way most people live just isn't working? How do we get this full life—the one that is "perissos"?

I've felt a shift in our culture lately where people are sick of just getting by. We've had enough of 9-to-5 jobs at coffee shops or cubicles where we just punch the time card. That life is easy, but not very fulfilling. It's the wide gate that most people choose. But most of us want something bigger; we want the life that is the right kind of full; packed with things that matter—things that have a lasting influence that outlive ourselves. Like Henry David Thoreau in his journey to Walden Pond, we yearn to "live deliberately... and not, when I came to die, discover that I had not lived."

In order to pursue that kind of life, we have to enter the narrow gate and do things very few people are willing to do.

Yolo.

Our culture today has a lot of rules that a lot of people agree on. You've probably heard things like, "Do whatever makes you happy." "If two consenting adults agree it's ok, it can't be wrong." "You only live once—YOLO!!"

Those little nuggets of wisdom might be popular, but they're the broad roads that lead to destruction. Just look at virtually any celebrity. *So many* of them struggle with drug and alcohol addiction, and it seems increasingly more are taking their own lives. Even with the "healthy" rock stars and actors featured on late night talk shows, can't you just tell by the look in their eyes that they're constantly and tirelessly fighting for relevance?

If you want a *full life* (not to be confused with a busy or prosperous one), we have to dare to make the tougher decisions on the narrow, more difficult roads.

The world around us is loudly shouting at us and telling us what is most important. We can't blindly obey. We need to step up and live with intentionality and challenge the culture around us if we desire the better path.

Upstream

I don't know much about fish. I'm pretty sure dolphins and whales are mammals, and one time I had a family of goldfish named after the Brady Bunch kids. That's pretty much the extent of my fish knowledge.

However, I do remember reading about a specific breed of salmon in science class. This one species of fish actually swims *upstream*, against the harsh and incredibly strong river current. These salmon take this upstream journey once in their lifetimes to mate before they die (might as well go out with a bang!). Some of these fish travel up to 7,000 miles (!) and it can take up to five years (!) to get to their final destination. During these trips, they somehow don't eat *anything* (!!!). One of the greatest mysteries of all is that these salmon navigate themselves back to the exact same stream where they were born to lay their eggs. Even though they typically migrate thousands of miles away during their lifetimes, somehow these fish literally fight and swim upstream back to their exact birthplace to have kids and die. There are a few theories out there about how exactly this happens (since fish don't generally have stellar internal GPS units), but scientists overall are baffled as to how accurate these journeys actually are.

They have to fight hard to survive this once-in-a-lifetime journey. Millions begin this migration pattern and only a few successfully hatch offspring. Science can't explain this instinct these fish have to fight upstream. It makes *no* sense. Their chances of survival would obviously be drastically higher if they laid eggs in calm water like virtually every other species of fish.

I don't need to draw the lines for you. Living

"upstream" and counter-culturally like Jesus taught is hard. It doesn't happen naturally; it requires years of intense hard work and struggle. Most people won't even try. Wide is the gate that leads to destruction, and many enter through it. But narrow is the road that leads to life, and only a few find it.

Millennials.

I wrote this book with millennials in mind for two reasons:

1) I am a millennial.

2) Simply slapping the word "millennial" on just about anything intended for a Christian audience will immediately double its sales, and I'm all about making money.

(If you're not a millennial, let me take a quick break to stress an important point right at the beginning: Most people my age are fluent in sarcasm. Please keep that in mind in the pages that follow.)

I believe the words and challenges in this book are true for everyone, no matter how old you are, but I have a strong passion to speak to the people of my generation. We have a chance to make a real difference. As we continue to age and gain influence, we can finally earn the platforms and experience we've been looking for to talk about and make changes to the things we're passionate about.

That's why every marketer is trying to get *you* to buy their product. That's why every politician is fighting for *your* vote. Money and votes spend and count the same regardless of age, but our culture is fighting hardest for *you* because you and

I are the future. What you and I believe is literally going to shape the world. This stuff is important and has significant implications.

A lot of the things I hear about millennials are not very nice. Older generations are fascinated by us and want to do whatever they can to figure us out, but I keep hearing all kinds of negative stereotypes. Millennials are leaving the church. Millennials are lazy and suffer with entitlement. Millennials care more about fashion and pop culture than they do about social justice. They're disrespectful and self-centered. They have crazy and radical views on marriage and relationships. They *all* voted for Obama, and look how *that* turned out!

(sarcasm)

Some of those things may be true, but I would argue that most of those claims aren't unique to my generation. We—as the humans species—are messed up and sinful. We do stupid things and all of us struggle with living outside of ourselves. I'm not convinced millennials are that much worse—or that much better—than any generation before or after us. Yes, some people my age are making poor decisions, but that's the wide gate. Yes, *most* people may be on that track, but it's possible to choose the narrow path, no matter what age bracket you find yourself in.

This life—this narrow road, this alternative to how everyone else is living—is admittedly much more difficult, but I believe it leads to "perissos" life. Throughout the rest of this book, each chapter addresses one specific issue that I think is important. In each case, there is one blatant message that our culture teaches is absolutely true and promises to lead to success and happiness. The more I thought and the more I studied the Bible, however, I've found that each time—with each important issue—the Bible often teaches the complete opposite message from what we hear in popular culture. Sometimes they don't literally contradict each other, but it became increasingly clear to me that the way Jesus taught us to live is radical and counter-cultural and requires us to swim against the cultural current. And that shouldn't surprise us either. A common theme of the Scriptures is that following Jesus *is* hard. Peter went as far as to call us "aliens and strangers" in this world (1 Peter 2:11). You *will* stand out as different, but I don't think it's a decision you'll regret.

Do you want perissos life? Do you want your days to matter? Do you want to devote your life to something larger than yourself? Let's go on this adventure together, and let's go upstream.

1 -- GREAT

I grew up watching a brilliant TV show called "Boy Meets World." Now, if you spend any time watching Disney Channel or Netflix, let me stress that I'm talking about "Boy Meets World" and not "Girl Meets World." Yes, some of the characters are the same, but let's get one thing straight; they are *very* different shows and one is significantly better than the other. If you or your kids prefer the new reboot, remind them to respect their elders.

(sarcasm)

Although the show was chock-full of great one-liners and the comedic brilliance that was the Feeny call, one of the final scenes of the show still vividly sticks with me today. Right before the gang leaves Mr. Feeny's classroom for the final time, America's favorite teacher/principal/professor/neighbor/gardener offers Cory, Shawn, and the rest of humanity one final Feeny-ism:

> Feeny: Believe in yourselves. Dream.
> Try. Do good.
> Topanga: Don't you mean, "Do well"?
> Feeny: No, I mean do *good*.

Ahhh. Doesn't that just send chills down your spine? You're a spry old sage, George Feeny!

"Well" measures success. "Good" measures our heart and our priorities, and Feeny wanted to make sure we knew which was more important before he left our airwaves for good.

People like me raised in this "Boy Meets World" generation also grew up in a culture that coached and inspired us to achieve greatness. Although many of us also struggle deep down with insecurity, we do believe in ourselves. We're not afraid to dream or try. In fact, we sometimes believe in ourselves to a fault. We think we can do whatever we want if we work hard enough. We may not verbalize it, but most of us see the success of LeBron James and Justin Bieber and other young superstars and think, "I could do that. I'm good enough to compete at their level. I have what it takes to be great. NBD."

Everyone is *good*. Good isn't good enough. Much like Topanga Lawrence in her insatiable desire for straight As, we yearn for *greatness*.

Just like Topanga attempted to educate George Feeny

about the difference between "well" and "good" (which was silly, because clearly Feeny knows everything) most of us make a similar argument about goodness vs. greatness. This underlying issue drove the plot of the Wizard of Oz reboot, "Oz: The Great and Powerful." After what we assume to be years of mediocrity, the struggling magician Oscar Diggs explains, "I don't want to be a good man... I want to be a *great* one." You can almost hear the years of pain and disappointment in his voice; the same pain that almost everyone in our generation feels as we get older.

We don't want to do well. Good isn't good enough. We need to be called *great*.

Good job.

A few years ago, I had the chance to apply for a job that made me feel great. A very large and very successful organization had an opening that at first glance seemed like a custom-fit for me. I went through the application process and ended up being one of their final two candidates. After a nationwide search of very qualified and unbelievably talented candidates, it was beginning to feel like this was it. This was my chance to show the world I was great. In all of my 24-year-old wisdom, I told myself I had worked long enough at a *good* job. I was ready for something *great*. I was ready to *arrive*.

(Roll of the eyes) typical millennial.

By the end of my final interview, I was well aware that I was not ready for the job. I'm good at what I do and I probably would have done well in the role, but it wasn't right at that time for several reasons. One of them, even though I didn't want to admit it, was my attitude and my perspective.

21

The dream of a cool title at a successful company inspired me to show off the best I had to offer.

The company I was applying for did a lot of good things. They help and serve thousands of people around the world. Although I was excited about joining a *good* company, my desire for greatness outweighed my desire for goodness.

Our culture today (probably more than ever before) idolizes young success stories. We love Mark Zuckerberg and Blake Mycoskie (the creator of TOMS Shoes) and Justin Timberlake and the like. If we are young and talented but have yet to be on the cover of Wired or GQ, it's strangely easy to feel like a failure. We feel like something is wrong with us if we don't have a billion Twitter followers and the little blue checkmark by our name. We should be better than this, we think. By now we should be better than ourselves.

Interestingly enough, many great people aren't very good, and many very good people aren't very great.

The more we focus on wealth and fame and success and pleasure, the less we tend to focus on our spouses and our children and our communities—and even ourselves.

As a Christian, I follow a Man who made radical claims like "The last will be first, and the first will be last" (Matthew 20:16). The "last" are often the ones who strive for goodness; most of the "firsts" strive for greatness.

Competition.

"Great" is way more competitive than "good."
Everyone can be good. Most of the time, only one person gets

to be great.

When I think about greatness, the first people that come to mind are athletes and music artists. People like Michael Jordan, Tom Brady, Michael Jackson, Whitney Houston, the Beatles—they were *great*, right? These people were arguably the best to ever do their professions. For future generations, every new success story will forever be compared to these greats. Kids around the world dream about being "the next" great superstar.

The list of greats is incredibly small.

After the Super Bowl, the winning team usually goes to Disney World and the White House and probably has a parade somewhere, but then what do they do? They go back to the gym. They watch film. They study what they did right and wrong in the last game they played. And soon, they go back to training camp, which most NFL players *hate* because it's hard, monotonous work. Very few players retire after winning the Super Bowl. After a few days or weeks of celebration, they go back to work and devote all of their time to try to win again next year. Why is that?

Greatness has a very short expiration date.

In my generation, the NFL really is the pinnacle of pop culture entertainment. There are very few events that such a huge percentage of our population watches at the same time. When I used to live in Colorado, there was *absolutely zero* traffic on the streets when the Broncos were playing. Even if you don't care about the actual game, just about everyone in America could probably recognize Tom Brady.

Let's look deeper at the Super Bowl—this game that almost everyone watches and advertisers pay *millions* to get our attention during. Even if you consider yourself an avid football fan, can you name the last three teams to win the Super Bowl? Can you name the last three teams to win the NCAA basketball tournament? Or the World Series? Did you know there's actually an NBA team named *The Pelicans*?! I'm not sure I could tell you with absolute certainty *anyone* who won a Grammy or an Academy Award last year.

Greatness is reserved for a select few, and we forget their names even a few years after their crowning life achievements. Great is exhausting, and you never really reach the goal because there is always more greatness to achieve.

Good.

This isn't true with good. Doing good makes you feel good. Doing great gives you a temporary high, but it quickly fades when someone else does something great. Doing something good has a longer lasting impact on your emotions, plus it usually ends up making others feel good, too.

One of my favorite movies is "The Pursuit of Happyness" starring Will Smith. Every time I watch it, I feel good. The main character overcomes incredible odds and reaches his (very humble) dreams by working hard to provide for his family. The movie ends with a guy getting a job—overall a fairly mundane climax to a movie. But that final scene with Will Smith clapping his hands out of pure joy in the crowd of hundreds of people in New York—that scene gives me chills every time. I feel good. After a good deed, both parties feel good.

At the end of every sports event, one team feels great and the other team feels horrible. There's something different about watching and witnessing good compared to watching and witnessing something great.

Momma's boys.

In the book of Matthew, we get a really interesting look at how Jesus views greatness. In chapter 20, the mother of James and John (two of the 12 disciples) comes to Jesus with a request:

> "Grant that one of these two sons of mine may
> sit at your right and the other at your left in
> your kingdom." (Matthew 20:21)

First of all, can we just acknowledge the awkwardness that these guys' *mom* comes and asks this of Jesus, the Savior of the world? Could there be *anything* more embarrassing? Talk about a momma's boy! In my mind, I can't help but see these guys roll their eyes and yell "Moooooooooomm!!" like any embarrassed teenager would.

Jesus responds and says they have no idea what they are asking. This overzealous soccer mom wanted her two baby boys to forever be considered great, sitting next to Jesus' throne for all of eternity. This would, of course, be a significant honor, reserved only for the greatest of men to ever live on earth. Jesus' next words are among my favorite verses in the Bible:

> "You know that the rulers of the Gentiles lord it
> over them, and their high officials exercise
> authority over them. Not so with you. Instead,

whoever wants to become great among you must
be your servant, and whoever wants to be first
must be your slave—just as the Son of Man did
not come to be served, but to serve, and to give
His life as a ransom for many."
(Matthew 20:25-28)

Drop the mic.

What a *good* response. You want your boys to be
considered great, overzealous soccer mom? Tell James and
John to do good. Stop trying to be in first place. Go help some
people and serve, just like Jesus did.

Jesus gives an important comparison in His response.
Most leaders in that day—just like *our* day—took advantage of
their authority. Many employers don't treat their workers very
well. Some parents are harsh to their children. A lot of leaders
pass along hard work they don't want to do to people ranked
lower than them. They expect to be served and pampered and
adored. That's what *most* leaders do. That's the wide road that
most people follow. What does Jesus say in response to that
reality? Four important words:

"Not so with you."

If we call ourselves Jesus followers, we're supposed to
go upstream. We can't follow the pack, because that's not the
kind of leadership our Savior modeled for us. Everyone else
may be caught up in the corporate rat race, but that lifestyle
isn't fulfilling. Chasing greatness leads to a temporary
emotional high that quickly fades. People forget your name and
you have to go back to training camp. It's an endless cycle that
leads to disappointment and destruction.

The rest of the world may never understand, but let's be a generation that yearns to do good instead of being great. Everyone else will tirelessly chase greatness, but not so with you. Never make excuses for poor work and continue to be the best at what you do. But at the same time, remember to use your skills and gifts on things that matter. Deep down, I think you know that this kind of life is more meaningful.

Besides. As a rule of thumb, it's generally a good idea to take advice from Mr. Feeny.

2 -- BIG

We all have an urge somewhere deep within us that yearns for growth. If nothing in our lives ever changed, even the laziest of people would eventually become incredibly bored. For you, maybe it's the size of your closet, the prestige associated with your job, or maybe even your high score on Candy Crush. Whatever it is, we all quickly tire of what we've already achieved.

Of course this can be either a really good trait, or a really bad one. We can use our drive and determination to better ourselves and add value to our communities, or we can waste that ambition on things that—if we're honest—don't really have any inherent value. We often applaud and reward the hard working ambitious leaders, but what if there is actually a danger in this desire for growth and the ever-moving target of "more"? What if "bigger" isn't always a healthy goal?

Child Size

In one of my favorite episodes of NBC's "Parks and Recreation," local congresswomen Leslie Knope urges her local town of Pawnee, Indiana to take steps toward healthier lifestyles. Her message was timely since their town motto was "First in friendship, fourth in obesity."

The pride of Indiana, I'm sure.

A local fast food joint in Pawnee had recently changed their "small" sodas to be a whopping 64 oz. and their "regular" to 128 oz. (also known as a gallon). And finally, news spread that they now offered a new "child-size" (512 oz.) cup, appropriately named since it is roughly the size of the average two-year-old child.

In Pawnee and the rest of America, we love big.

I work at a church that I would label "medium-sized." Our congregation has grown in recent years, and it is tempting for us to always be on the lookout for the next secret ingredient that can push us toward some sort of new attendance milestone. Of course I desire for more and more people in our community to take steps of growth in their walk with Christ, and it would be great if we saw a huge influx of guests searching for a church home. However, sometimes when I hear some people—myself included—dreaming up new techniques for us to reach new audiences, something just feels... icky. Out of place. Fake.

Too big.

We *could* try hosting a car show or have an incredible

Fourth of July fireworks show. We *could* rent a billboard and use suggestive and shocking marketing lingo. We *could* have a waterfall on our stage and hire a stunt motorcycle driver to do crazy fire jumps following our announcements.

We *could* do all sorts of things (and all of those things *have* been done at churches), but those don't feel natural for *us*. Maybe things like that can be effective in some contexts, but in our community with our collection of attenders and our staff, it would feel forced, unnatural, and unnecessary.

We may get more people to attend for a season, but after a while they would realize that we aren't really the billboard church we advertised. We don't have fireworks every week. That's not what we do well, and that's not who we are.

The talents

In the book of Matthew, there is a really fascinating story that has come to be known as the parable of the talents. In it, Jesus tells a story about a very wealthy man who entrusted various sums of money to his three servants while he was out of town. Two of the three servants made wise investments and doubled their amounts, while the third man did nothing and returned the money to his master with zero interest.

Of course the third man who made no money is frowned upon. He was scared and lazy. He literally dug a hole and put the money underground so he wouldn't lose it. Real winner. If I had to guess, I'd say he probably lived in his parents' basement and played a lot of video games. I bet he aced his personal finance class in high school, too. Compound interest, you fool!

(sarcasm)

The money in this story is measured in a currency called "talents." A talent in that day was *a lot of money*. Modern estimates guess that a talent was worth approximately *20 years of labor*, so one talent was worth at least $300,000 by today's standards. Matthew tells us this third servant who didn't make any profit was given one talent, so it would have been fairly easy for him to at least put the talent in a bank and earn interest. When the wealthy man returns and finds that he didn't even do that, the master takes back the man's talent—the only one he was given—and gives it to the most successful man who now has 11 talents.

The lesson is clear: Be a good steward of what you have. Work hard. Don't be lazy. Understand basic investing strategies. Don't hide your money in the mud.

At first glance, it appears that more really is better.

Those are all valuable lessons, for sure, but something else in this story catches my eye. There's one thing I didn't mention before: The two men who made profits on their talents were given different amounts to begin with. One was given five talents, and the other was given two. Both of them made wise investments and doubled their money. Yes, the man who earned five talents was given more in the end, but what's interesting to me is that the lender gave the exact same response to these two men:

> "Well done, good and faithful servant. You have been faithful over a little; I will set you over much. Enter into the joy of your master." (Matthew 25:23)

Putting the amounts of money aside for a moment, both men were rewarded. The master was proud and offered praise to both of them. This man, who represents Jesus, isn't overly impressed with the servant who gained five talents. With the information we have, I would assume the master would have passed along a similar praise and blessing to the man with one talent if he had doubled his investment and ended up with two. He doesn't chastise the second man for only gaining two. In his mind, both men were successful and therefore entrusted with more responsibility. In modern language, the small business was treated the same as the corporation. The community church was granted the same favor as the megachurch.

For the sake of story, I see myself as the man who was given two talents. I don't think of myself as particularly noteworthy, and I don't have a track record of incredible success. But, to my credit, I also don't hide my money in the mud.

You know yourself. You know your business or your family or your church or your classroom. You want growth and improvement, and you know your culture. If you're a medium church and want to be a large church, don't immediately start acting like a big church.

For *our* church where I work, I knew we were a pretty good medium church. We weren't *really* good yet. My team and I knew we could get better at the areas we were good at and improve on our weaknesses before we completely changed our evangelism and outreach strategies. Before hosting huge events and inviting A-list speakers and probably using a fog machine, we needed to work on having a better church bulletin. Our website was awful. We had no signage in our church telling people where the nursery was.

We needed to gain two more talents, not five. And that's ok.

Toothpaste

When I was in second or third grade, I wrote my first book. I don't really remember what it was about, but I know it included a lot of Microsoft clipart, and I'm fairly certain the protagonist made toothpaste. My dad was my publisher, and I remember we went to some printing store to give it special binding on shiny paper.

I've always enjoyed writing, and my high school newspaper gave me my first real shot at being published. Instead of documenting the toothpaste creation process that I almost certainly made up, one of my most popular columns made fun of our local weatherman. I also pleaded with the school district to give us more snow days, and I complained quite extensively about my discontent with changes made in Halo 2 for XBox.

I tackled the real issues of our day. And people thought I was hilarious.

(sarcasm)

After on-again-off-again-attempts at maintaining a blog, a couple years ago I decided I wanted to really branch out and show the world my talent. It was time for the world to read my witty and insightful cultural commentary.

As all successful authors do, I wrote up a few posts and

sent them directly to the editor of a handful of my favorite magazines. Nationwide, big, trendy, successful magazines you've heard of.

And then I waited. Like two days.

I kept my email inbox open and occasionally hit refresh.

Nothing came. And I was heartbroken.

Amazingly, my jump from high school journalist to nationally syndicated columnist wasn't as easy as I anticipated. I wasn't ready to be *big* yet, and thank goodness they didn't publish the trash I sent those magazines.

The Roadmap

In his book, *Start,* Jon Acuff documents a "roadmap to success." He claims we all have to go through the five-step process of learning, editing, mastering, harvesting, and guiding. Harvesting is where we all want to be. That stage is where you enjoy success and all the benefits that come with it after years of hard work.

When I first started submitting my articles to whoever would listen a few years ago, I was not in that stage yet. I had learned some skills and even refined my passions, but I was (and still am) *far* from mastering my craft. I tried to skip over that "mastering" step, and it's a pretty significant one. It's where you hustle, work hard, and really refine your skills. It's where you actually become good at something. You hone in on your greatest gifts, talents, and passions, and do the hard work required to enter into harvesting.

So many celebrities in our culture today got their start by

being noticed on YouTube or winning "American Idol," so we begin to think that we also have what it takes to be an overnight success. Why bother with the hours and days and years of hard work when a couple of lucky breaks could land us in the national spotlight? Surely if we post a few witty tweets, open up an Etsy shop, or dream up a Kickstarter campaign, we'll instantly have all the money and success of our wildest dreams!

This is America, right? 'Murica!

After the punch in the gut pride-check I experienced after my first several publishing attempts, I decided to take a different approach. Instead of attempting to jump from high school journalist to distinguished magazine columnist, I wrote on my blog. I'd get a few hits here and there, but my audience was *very* small. Once I had a decent collection of posts, I sent a link to the editor of my church denomination's magazine. It was a nationwide publication, but it was sent to a very small, niche market of my peers. They were looking for content, and I was looking for a platform. They gave me a chance, and my first piece was published.

After a few pieces published with this magazine (and several more rejection emails from others), one day I decided to give it a shot one more time, and I sent a column to my favorite magazine. I didn't hear anything for a few days, and I honestly began to forget about it. I assumed the silence just meant yet another "No."

But then, on one glorious Thursday, the stars aligned and I read a different word in my email inbox. After all those failed attempts, *finally* the editor let me know they enjoyed my perspective and the article was already published on their website.

Of course, I played it cool, shrugged it off and went back to digging holes for my borrowed $300,000.

... ARE YOU KIDDING ME?

My face couldn't help but smile for hours! I frantically went and told the story to co-workers who probably thought I drank something crazy on my lunch break. I immediately texted anyone I could think of and posted the link all over any section of the Internet I had any control over. *That* feeling is what I worked hard for, but it certainly didn't come without years of growth and a lot of "no's."

Don't email me.

Since I'm involved in marketing and content creation, I read and study a lot of leaders who talk about how to get your message to a large audience. If you write a book, have an idea for a screen play, an item to pitch on "Shark Tank," or really any *thing* that you want to be *big*, there are people all over the Internet who have strategies to follow to make it possible. They make it sound really easy.

A lot of these people have really great things to say, but I also disagree with some of the things marketing gurus suggest. Just about all of them will tell you that the key to a large audience is to have a large email list. Many of today's best marketers have lists of thousands of people who signed up for an email newsletter, and they regularly send big blasts letting these people know about their latest product, podcast, blog post, online course, or opportunity to get involved.

These guys obviously know what they're talking about, but for me there was just one problem: *I hate email.* I'm one of those annoying OCD people who have to keep their inboxes at 0. (If you're one of those horrible people who constantly have 4,326 unread emails on your phone, *please get help.*) When I get messages from businesses I shopped at once three years ago, I get mad and instantly unsubscribe. If I somehow get subscribed to some newsletter that I've never heard of, I immediately get a bad taste in my mouth about that company. Even with organizations that I like and respect, I only want to hear from them if it's something really important to me.

My point is this: be yourself. Don't do things that feel weird to you simply to become bigger or better or to gain more followers. Growing, getting better and *bigger* can be a good goal. Just don't rush the process. Don't aim for big simply because it feels like you have to or you feel unsuccessful if you're in a small or medium phase of life. Embrace the number of talents you have, and then get to work. There's not actually anything wrong with "big," but there may be something wrong if that is your only goal.

The rest of the world is tirelessly fighting for big promotions, massive nationwide platforms, instant celebrity, and all the accolades that come with those things. Let's go upstream. Work hard and dream big, but keep your priorities in check and remember to embrace (and enjoy) the process.

3 -- BUSY

If smart phones have taught us anything, it's that "more" is always possible. It's getting harder and harder to completely disengage from work and unplug from people constantly requesting increased production.

For people like me in the emerging generation, many of us told ourselves we would never be like the workaholics we've seen come before us. Remember Arnold Schwarzenegger's character in "Jingle All the Way"? He missed his son Jamie's karate lesson to work late at the office. AND HE FORGOT TO GET A TURBO MAN ACTION FIGURE. (rolling eyes emoji)

What an *awful* parent. I vowed I would never become *that* Schwarzenegger. A different Schwarzenegger? Maybe. But only because of our similar physical physique.

Now with a few years of real world experience under my

belt, those decisions about balancing work and family are much harder than I realized. I love my wife and treasure my time with her, but sometimes it's not possible to *not* finish that work project. Sometimes we *have* to keep an eye on email late at night and on the weekends.

Our culture always pushes for more—and not just in the workplace. Remember when Michael Jordan retired from basketball—again—in the late 90s? After he retired, I'm sure many people told him he still had more left in his tank. He was the undisputed best player to ever play the game. He had all the accolades athletes strive for (and by that, of course, I mean he starred in a full-length feature film alongside Bugs Bunny).

He could have called it quits at the peak of sports and cultural achievement, but instead he listened to the voices asking for more, and he played for the Washington Wizards.

It didn't go so well.

Just ask Brett Favre.

For all you non-sports fans out there, go watch the *fourth* Indiana Jones movie. Or did you know there was a "Caddyshack 2"? How could we forget "I *Still* Remember What You Did Last Summer"?

More is not always better.

Math

I'm not great at math or science, but it makes sense to me that the process of creating something new requires a transfer of energy. You can't make something from nothing. Even if you're simply coming up with an idea, that thing came from somewhere. Some of *you* is released with every new idea and project you create. At some point, we have to refill and refuel if we hope to maintain our sanity and our creativity. Or as Blaine Hogan says, before an artist can move others, the artist must first be moved.

So why is it that we keep pushing forward and starve ourselves of rest? Why is it *so hard* to turn the phone off and simply exist without distractions? Why is "more" such an addicting idea? Why is everyone always so stinkin' busy?

Aunt May

Deep down, *busy* makes us feel valuable. Everyone can do a normal amount of work; we want to be *more*. We fear that living a "normal" life isn't good enough. If we don't do more, we could be replaced. Someone else out there could be better. It hurts to admit it, but part of our identity and pride stem from our ability to do multiple things well. If we can't handle more, it means we are less.

We equate busy-ness with value.

In the "Amazing Spider-Man 2" movie, there is one beautiful exchange between Peter Parker and his Aunt May. After a brief argument, Aunt May begins to unload on Peter about all of the sacrifices she has made for him. She adopted him as a child and put her life on hold to give this fatherless boy a chance. She tearfully admits that she's taking on a second job to help him pay for college, and you can tell she's about to completely lose it when Peter interrupts.

"That's enough. You're *more* than enough."

41

Goose bumps.

I can't help but see the spiritual parallels here. I sometimes see myself in Aunt May, on the verge of tears, telling God that I keep working overtime, I take on additional freelance jobs, I joined a worship team, I strive to be a good husband, and on and on my list continues. I'm so *busy*. Can't you see my value?

Jesus stops me, looks in my eyes, and tells me I'm enough.

Take it easy. Breathe. Turn off the phone.

There's no need to strive for more. He won't think any less of us. In fact, He calls us to less.

WWJD

I wonder if Jesus ever struggled with this "busy" addiction. He frequently went away to rest by Himself, but He could have used that time to heal more people. He could have traveled further distances to tell His story to new regions. He didn't run out of miracles. There was more water to walk on and other parties that could use adult beverages. Do you think He ever struggled with guilt over not doing more?

I don't know. Either way, Jesus recognized that His humanity demanded rest. Being God Himself, He probably could have tapped into an energy source we don't have (or invented Red Bull a few centuries early), but maybe He also rested to give us an example.

We need to do our jobs well. As Christians, we can't be known as slackers unwilling to finish the job. But, we also can't run ourselves into the ground. More is not always better. Being busy doesn't make us more valuable. Listen to the voice of the One who knit you together:

> "Come to me, all you who are weary and
> burdened, and I will give you rest. Take my yoke
> upon you and learn from me, for I am gentle
> and humble in heart, and you will find rest for
> your souls." (Matthew 11:28-29)

(Confession: Sometimes when I'm reading, I don't actually read every sentence or paragraph. If I think I already know what someone is going to say, sometimes I stop listening. I'm guessing some of you didn't read that paragraph because you've read it before. Busted! Go back and read it. Stop being too busy to read.)

Now, those words are refreshing, aren't they?

Put down the phone.

There's no need to watch "Caddyshack 2."

Read this chapter a little slower. No one's timing you.

Take some time to just *be*. What you're doing is enough. Make a conscious effort to learn from Him and find rest for your soul.

Eat Pray Love

Elizabeth Gilbert wrote a bestselling book called *Eat Pray Love*. Not only was it a popular book, but it was also made into a full-feature movie starring Julia Roberts. I think it's safe to say that you've officially "made it" when you get to work with any team member from "Ocean's 11."

Because of that success, Elizabeth was offered all sorts of opportunities and accolades that most of us will probably never have the burden of experiencing. You know, like wealth and influence and being on Oprah. I'm guessing she and Julia get together to play bridge over coffee once a month. You know, normal celebrity stuff.

(sarcasm)

While all of that may (or may not) be true, Elizabeth has also learned some important lessons while learning to deal with this new lifestyle. The following is an excerpt from a post on her Facebook page:

> I was thinking today about all the other paths that I did not take in life, no matter how shiny and appealing they may have looked. I've had the possibility of living so many different kinds of life that could have been a dream for somebody else. I never chose those lives. I've never lived the dreams that other people wanted for themselves — nor have I lived the dreams that other people may have wanted for me.
>
> I never had children...because that's somebody else's dream.
>
> I never took the opportunities that were offered to me after the success of *Eat Pray Love* to have a TV show of my own...because that's somebody else's dream.

I never took a good steady job teaching writing at a nice college...because that's somebody else's dream.

I didn't remain in Bali or Rome, gorgeous as those places are...because that's somebody else's dream.

I turn down 99% of the invitations I get to attend to fancy parties and stellar gatherings...because that's somebody else's dream.

I never hired a team of personal assistants and staff and consultants to help me "grow my brand"...because that's somebody else's dream.

I know what makes me come to life — working on my books ... Knowing what makes me come to life has helped me to distinguish between my dreams and the dreams of others.

In the world of *busy* and *more*, most of us struggle to know what really makes us come alive and what we just feel like we *should* do. If you read through that quote again, all of those things she turned down—having kids, owning a beautiful home, traveling overseas—at first glance, those sound like good things. Maybe even incredibly great things. But because those things didn't align with her dream, pursuing them led to exhaustion and unnecessary clutter in her life.

Instead, she took the narrower road and chose to focus on what brought her joy. We need to do the same.

I confess that this is super hard for me. My brain knows that it's not possible for me to be good at everything, but my heart just doesn't want to believe it. I put enormous pressure on myself to be successful at everything. The unfortunate reality is that when you do that, you end up doing hundreds of things with mediocrity instead of being really good at one or two things.

Companies, organizations, and churches are also bad at this. My pastor recently mentioned a blog post he read where the author explained how most successful churches do "less better." Instead of always trying to do more, they focus on a handful of things their church family is good at and passionate about. Is helping orphans in China a good thing? What about mentoring troubled teens in your community? Helping at a soup kitchen? Hosting a blood drive? Offering parenting classes? Social activities for disabled children?

You get it. The list of "good things" is incredibly long, and you can't do them all. Don't chase after things that aren't your dream or things you know you're not good at. Do less better, and then you just might make a difference.

My favorite vocabulary lesson

I had an English teacher in high school who (...or should that be whom?) had a reputation of being particularly tough. She was brilliant and taught me much of what I know about grammar, but her class was *hard*. We received college credit for taking it, and we earned every single stinkin' one of those three hours on our transcripts.

Every Friday in that class we had a vocabulary test. I remember every week I would receive the list of words and gawk at them wondering if they were, in fact, actual English words. Some of them were incredibly long words probably used by scientists in lab coats, some were technical jargon used in instruction manuals for assembling motorcycles, and some of them were just flat out ridiculous. I can safely say I haven't used very many of those words in this book or in my 10 years of life since that course.

My classmates and I liked to play a game where we would try to squeeze as many of these words as possible into made up sentences that probably didn't make any sense because we didn't actually know the definitions. One of those phrases that somehow got stuck in my brain was this:

Jettison the flotsam.

We thought we were hilarious just because that combination of consonants sounds silly, but I didn't realize how much of a philosopher I was being with that ridiculous phrase. In case you didn't take that course in high school or haven't spent any time at sea, "jettison" is a verb meaning to throwing something overboard from a ship, and "flotsam" is basically floating wreckage found in the ocean.

Amazingly that sentence actually works, but it's also relevant to this chapter. In this crazy, busy world, get rid of the wreckage. Toss it overboard. Make the load of your ship lighter by getting rid of the excess.

Jettison the flotsam.

Three things.

Donald Miller is one of my heroes. He is a terrific

writer, but I also get the sense that he just knows how to live a good life. In one of his recent writing projects, he explains that he aims to only take on three projects a year. Any more than that, and he'll be stretched too thin. This quote from Don is one of my favorites of all time:

> "You can either get a little bit done
> on a lot of projects or you can finish
> a few of them and change the world."

Most of my life, I've tried to do way more than three things at once. Every once in a while I experience moderate success, but I've also been tired. I feel out of balance. Like it could all crumble at any moment. It's a stressful and horrible feeling.

Another successful man, Warren Buffett, once said:

> "The difference between successful people and
> unsuccessful people is that really successful people say
> no to almost everything."

More is not always better.

Do less better.

Go upstream. Everyone else tries to do too much. Instead, do a few things really well.

Turn off your phone. Stop trying to do everything. Come to Jesus, all who are weary and burdened. Take some time to just *be*. Jettison the flotsam.

4 -- RELEVANT

One of the buzzwords that the church and the culture at large loves right now is "relevant." Everything has to be relevant. Whether people are selling cheese or dryer sheets or Christianity, I guarantee a bunch of guys in suits somewhere have used that word in marketing meetings. That is a good goal by definition, but we've taken it way too far. I can just imagine quotes being thrown around in those meetings:

> "I don't know, guys. We've just *got* to find a way to make Gouda relevant again."

> "I can't figure out why, but Tide is just *killing* the millennial market right now."

Social media is a great example of this (and we'll dive deeper in the next chapter). Since it is so popular in our world today, people are jumping in head first in ways that aren't helpful. There's one particular gas station I drive by fairly often that has a big marquee sign out front that simply says, "Like us on Facebook!"

Just a quick recap: a local *gas station* is inviting me to give them permission to invade my News Feed.

I've driven past it probably 400 times, and I can't tell you the name of the gas station. There's *no way* I'd be able to find it on Facebook if I tried. But even if I did, what *possible* value would that add to my life? At the very best, maybe I get one free coupon for a cheap hot dog, and then it just adds clutter to my News Feed for the rest of eternity. At the very worst, I'm imagining lots of horrible cat memes using Comic Sans and Papyrus.

Just because social media is popular and influential, would you call that gas station "relevant"? I'm definitely not saying fringe (or mainstream, for that matter) markets can't be successful with social media, but they definitely won't be if they have shaky intentions and poorly planned strategies. If your only goal is "relevance," you will likely fail and people will forget the name of your gas station.

Whether we talk about politicians, pastors, or any other leaders in our culture today, a lot of them chase relevance in a way that forces them to morph their personalities. I can't be the only one who has seen a pastor *waayyyy* too old to be wearing skinny jeans also walking around with an iPad, cup of trendy fair-trade coffee, that weird half-shaved-half-combover haircut, and saying strange things like "totes mcgoates."

If we ever meet, please never say totes mcgoates.

Or you've probably seen an older presidential candidate that suddenly realizes he needs to reach college students, so he shows up on the "The Tonight Show" and plays a goofy game with Jimmy Fallon that just feels uncomfortable to everyone.

Can we just... stop? Please?

Current.

Let's pause for a moment and talk about what "relevant" means. I once heard an important story from a pastor who asked his congregation to tweet in questions or feedback during his Sunday sermon. He put a hashtag up on the screen and went on to give his normal talk. At the end of the morning, he was shocked and heartbroken to see that he didn't get *any* responses.

How could this be?! Was his sermon that horrible? Were people sleeping? Was the church wifi down? Maybe the Twitter Fail Whale had struck again?

No. He got zero responses because he didn't know his audience. This particular church was mostly middle-aged adults several years ago before hashtags were everywhere. Nobody in his church knew what the pound sign was doing all over his PowerPoint, much less what they were supposed to do with it. Somebody probably asked him later what he was talking about when he mentioned "The Tweeter."

This pastor—like so many of us—confused "relevant" with "current." Twitter was current, but in his culture in his context, it was *not* relevant.

Relevant does not mean trendy. Relevant does not mean

cutting-edge. Relevant does not mean whatever twentysomethings are doing today. "Relevant" means "having significant and demonstrable bearing on the matter at hand." If people don't know how to demonstrate what you're talking about, you're not being relevant.

Bluetooth man.

If you'll allow me to be blunt for a moment: The truth is that many of our leaders today—inside and outside the church—aren't current. They probably have belt clips for their phones and walk around using Bluetooth headsets. If that's you—and you're doing it because you really like it—just... rock it, man. Go for it. But if you're doing those things in an attempt to be relevant, I hate to be the one to tell you that it isn't working. Not only is it not working, but the people you're trying to reach are probably laughing at you.

And honestly, that's ok, cell-phone-holster-man. I applaud you for your desire to swiftly answer a call at the speed of light any time you feel a slight vibration or obnoxiously loud ring tone (*much* faster than silly people like me who have to *dig in our pockets* to get our phones). You probably won't connect with me or my friends very effectively, but maybe you will reach other cell-phone-holster-people, and they need saved just as badly as my millennial friends.

An argument could be made that they need to be saved even faster.

(sarcasm)

Before this sounds like too much of an old-person-bash, let me be clear: people of all ages are guilty of this. In fact, we all are. Deep down (some of us deeper than others), we are insecure. Part of being human means that we have a need for inclusion and belonging. If we're a part of a conversation or in a social setting where we're afraid we may not fit in, most of us default to trying to use social cues to blend in. I can't even tell you how many times in junior high and high school I fake lip-synced along with songs on the radio when driving with my friends (using the tried-and-true "watermelon, watermelon" approach, of course). My parents were strict on what movies I could see growing up, so I often found myself quoting famous film sequences that I had never seen and had zero context for. I'm pretty sure I had most of "Ace Ventura: Pet Detective" memorized before I ever saw it. I did anything I could to appear current, even when I had no idea what I was talking about.

Am I the only one who did that? Didn't think so.

Just be weird.

God wired each of us to be unique. I'm great at some things and horrible at most other things. You may have a skill set that is literally the complete opposite of mine, and I think that's awesome. *No one* is good at every thing all the time right away. (And thank goodness. If that guy had a bad day or made a deal with the Decepticons, we'd all be in trouble.)

Not only do we all have different gifts and skills, but we all also have quirks. In a moment of completely honest self-reflection, just admit it: you are weird. You probably hide it, but there is *something* you do that most of the rest of us don't do.

For me, I have a very irrational dislike of any movie that

takes place in the 1800s featuring people speaking in British accents. I have *no* reasoning behind it and I honestly can't explain it. I know; it's weird. I just don't understand how you can make a complete PBS Masterpiece series about a girl named "Downtown Abbie."

For the first few months of my marriage, my wife made fun of me profusely when she learned that I fold my socks and underwear when doing the laundry. She does the apparently "normal" thing where you turn your socks inside out in pairs and just throw your undies in the drawer. She could not get over how weird I was for laying my socks in piles and neatly folding them together. It's (apparently) weird.

I love to exercise and run. But you know what else? I also love pizza and Mountain Dew. It is definitely not that uncommon for me to run four or five or six miles and then come home and just completely go nuts on food that more than cancels out any progress I just made on my workout.

That last one may not be weird as much as it is stupid, but you get the point. I'm weird.

My wife Tillie is a perfect model of weird. I absolutely love her more than anything in the world, and she is one of the most likable people you'll ever meet. But, she is different. It is not at all uncommon for us to be somewhere with dozens of people who could potentially be watching us and she'll just break into song and dance. *Weird* song and dance. Without any context, she'll just start groovin' away to commercial jingles or Disney soundtracks or pop songs from the 80s that I've never heard.

Just... because!

You may not dance to local window installment company's commercials in the aisles of Lowes, but each of us is weird. Obviously there are some social standards that are helpful for us to stick to, but it can also be exhausting to hide who you really are or force yourself to change to fit in with a specific crowd.

I still fold my socks.

I *always* fall asleep during the "Lord of the Rings" movies.

(In my mind I'm dodging hundreds of tomatoes that you all are throwing at me for that last one)

Plus, an added bonus for us alive right now is that it's cool to be weird. I mean, have you seen "Portlandia"?

Get real.

The opposite (and healthier) alternative to chasing relevance is embracing your reality. Just be real. No more hiding and no more faking. Being real and being relevant are both good goals, but neither will be effective if your motives aren't pure. If you act current to appear relevant, people will notice. If you pretend to be real to manipulate people, the truth will come out. Whether you're a marketing executive trying to sell cheese or an elementary teacher dancing in the aisles like my wife, just be the best version of yourself you can be. Don't obsess over being current. Be you, and be you well. We need more people like that today.

There has been a new trend in advertising lately that focuses on this idea of being real. Instead of simply talking up a new product or gadget, a lot of ads today choose to tell stories. Instead of trying to make us laugh with talking frogs and guys getting hit in the crotch, more and more companies are pulling at our heart strings by telling cute stories about kids and their dads, or reminding us about a simpler time in American history before the world got so cluttered, or even the longer Budweiser commercials featuring puppies on "Homeward Bound"-esque journeys beating all odds to be reunited with their owners. A growing percentage of Super Bowl ads feature some kind of cute or inspiring story like this—sometimes up to two or three minutes long—and then suddenly the story gets neatly wrapped with a corporate logo.

I have to admit that I miss the stupid humor I used to look forward to on Super Bowl Sunday, but on one hand I can appreciate what these companies are doing. In a way, they're complimenting their audiences. They're saying that we, as a culture, have evolved past the cheesy low-brow humor of talking babies and instead are choosing to invest in telling stories that are more relatable to our deepest longings and desires.

I love and appreciate beauty and creative storytelling, but you may be surprised to hear that these ads really bother me. Hear me out.

Let's focus on one specific ad so we're all on the same page. In the 2015 Super Bowl, Toyota released one ad titled "My Bold Dad"; a real tear-jerker showing a father sticking up for his daughter in a variety of big life moments before finally dropping her off at the airport to apparently join the military. They share one final teary goodbye before she walks away into the proverbial sunset, leaving good ol' pops alone in the pretty

red Camry. Next frame? "The bold new Camry. Toyota. Let's
Go Places."

The beauty of telling a great story is diminished when
you end it with your shiny logo. Now, instead of wanting to be
a good dad, I'm a little confused about the motive of the ad.
What is the call to action? What is supposed to be the
takeaway? Am I supposed to invest in my family, or buy a new
car? Am I supposed to buy a Toyota instead of a Ford because
of this one-minute story?

I don't think I'm really all that jaded. I hope I'm not
overly skeptical, but knowing what I do about advertising and
past experience with capitalism, this ad leaves me with a lot of
questions, and frankly none of them are about my father
(Sorry, dad). Maybe Toyota really does care about dads taking
steps to be better parents, but at the end of the day, they're
trying to get me to buy a car. I watch a lot of TV and
frequently listen to the radio. Every day other than Super Bowl
Sunday, Toyota's ads simply feature the latest features of the
latest Corola. I'm sure they have some kind of community
giving back program where they give a lot of money to charity,
but I don't think I've ever stopped to notice and appreciate
anything Toyota has done to make a real difference in my life.
Sure, a cute story about dads is nice, but it seems out of place
when we only hear that message once a year while our airwaves
are flooded with advertising messages the rest of the year.

Real is consistent. Current follows trends.

Did they make that ad to be real, or did they do it to be
current? Are they really trying to change how our country
views parenthood, or are they trying to garner social media
buzz and claim spots on top ten lists? Did they take this

approach because it's perceived to be an effective advertising strategy, or do they actually care about my family?

Eat more chicken.

In my community, there is one company that I think has mastered this concept and has modeled how I wish everyone would run their business. My friend Jason is the owner of a local Chick-Fil-A franchise. Of course they make a great chicken sandwich, but this little fast food restaurant is so much bigger than a simple value meal.

Jason and his wife Linda are very active at our church. Just about any time we host an event, Jason and Linda are there with handfuls of free sandwich coupons. At our Halloween Trunk or Treat event, Jason hired some of his employees to come to the event dressed in cow costumes to dance in the parking lot with children. He treats (and pays) his employees very well. One time I heard one of his workers say he gave them each stacks of gift cards and encouraged his workers to give them away to any friends or family who were in need. His management team does community service projects together. Whenever they donate food or prize packages, they refuse to get any recognition or public praise. Every year they host a Daddy Daughter Date night—in Chick-Fil-A—where dads are encouraged to dress up in nice clothes and bring their little princesses to a candle-lit dinner, complete with fancy music, a photo booth, and frilly decorations that Jason and Linda spend *weeks* preparing for. There is no additional cost above the normal price for a sandwich and kids meal.

Toyota spent millions on one commercial that aimed to elicit an emotional one-minute response.

Chick-Fil-A actively cares for my community and tangibly offers opportunities for families to grow together.

Which of these two companies feels real to you, and which one is chasing relevance? When this "real" storytelling fad fades—and it will—what kinds of ads will Toyota be making then?

I have nothing against Toyota. I'm sure lots of good people work there. However, I'm a brand advocate for Chick-Fil-A. More than just good food, they're making a real, practical, hands-on difference. I don't question their motives when they talk about the value of faith and family; they live it out every day.

Paul indirectly addressed this subject in his letter to the Galatians:

"Am I now trying to win the approval of human beings, or of God? Or am I trying to please people? If I were still trying to please people, I would not be a servant of Christ." (Galatians 1:10)

Most of the time, being relevant is about pleasing others. The Bible is full of verses that are very clear that God created you uniquely on purpose. You—the *real* you—have specific purposes ordained by God. So be who God made you to be. Be real. Be a servant of Christ, not of relevance.

Remember, there's nothing *bad* with "relevant"; in fact, it can be a very good thing. Our culture has just warped it. Instead of tirelessly pursuing relevance, we should simply be real. Be ourselves. No more faking to fit in. Instead of relevant, be real. And being real usually means being weird.

60

5 -- SOCIAL

When it comes to advances in media and technology, I'm an early adopter. Out of the 2,000 students who went to my high school, I was the second kid to get an iPod. *Years* before the first iPhone or iPad, this was simply a hunk of metal and plastic that played music. It wasn't even a cool Nano that could shoot video or a Shuffle you could clip to your pocket; I'm talking the *original* iPod with a 20 gig hard drive. Black and white. No touch screen. No videos or photos, but there were four little buttons above the scroll wheel.

Kids these days don't know how good they have it.

When I showed this remarkable new device to my high school friends, everyone laughed at me. "*Why* would you spend hundreds of dollars on something I can do on my $20 CD player?" they'd say with a scoff. "*Why* do you need to have *all* of your songs with you *all the time?*" they'd ask.

I just sat back with my pretty, white ear buds and smiled. I knew some day—one day—they would understand.

The same was true for me with social networks. I was among the first of my friends to have a Xanga. I could never push myself to actually pay for "Premium," but you better believe I spent a considerable amount of time choosing colors, coming up with clever things to say in my header, and even embedding mp3s of my favorite bands.

MySpace, Facebook, Twitter, Instagram, Foursquare, Google+, Justin Timberlake's "new" MySpace (remember that?)—you name it, I was among the first to adopt. I even scroll through Pinterest a few times a week. Go ahead, take away one of my Man Cards if you must.

It seems today there are basically two camps when it comes to social media: those who love it and post *ev. ery. thing.* they ever do or think (we get it... you love Pumpkin Spice Lattes), and those who—for one reason or another—either boycott it completely or make a conscience decision not to engage.

Wherever you stand, the dangers of social media have been appropriately documented in recent years. They definitely can cheapen human relationships, and it gives all of us access to a 24/7 feed of touched-up and filtered selfies to compare ourselves to. It truly is a completely different world than it was even a handful of years ago, and because of that, it's a topic worth discussing here. I'm guessing you've heard or read some of the common criticisms and complaints from social media haters, but I want to offer a hopefully unique perspective on how you can live upstream online.

Fruitless.

First things first, let's just address what we all already know: there's a lot of noise on social networks. It can be incredibly easy to get sucked into a strange time/space continuum where you look at the clock and realize you've spent 45 minutes creepin' on old high school friends, playing ridiculous farming games, or pinning hundreds of wooden headboards you know you'll never actually build.

In the book of Ephesians, Paul goes on a little rant in the fifth chapter. He writes out a list of things that the people in Ephesus (and us today) were supposed to avoid, and even goes a step further and says we should "have nothing to do with the fruitless deeds of darkness." He continues on in verses 15-17:

> "Be very careful, then, how you
> live—not as unwise but as wise,
> making the most of every
> opportunity, because the days are evil.
> Therefore do not be foolish, but
> understand what the Lord's will is."

If Paul were speaking these words today, I think we would sense a hint of frustration and even sarcasm in his voice. Allow me, if you will, to paraphrase:

> "Ain't nobody got time for that."

Take a quick pause from reading this. Go ahead and pull up your Facebook News Feed. What do you see? I'm guessing several selfies, maybe a couple quizzes about what "Mad Men" character you are, or maybe "What state you *should* have lived in." Several food photos. Someone is complaining about homework or their job. Others are sharing inspiring quotes or maybe even Bible verses. Somebody is probably making fun of Donald Trump's hair.

I would argue that social networks actually have immense value. But out of the things you just saw, was your life improved because of what you read? Were your relationships deepened and encouraged by those Buzzfeed links you scrolled past? Did anything you saw add value to your life, or were they merely "fruitless deeds"? Did that time help or hurt our mandate to "make the most of every opportunity"?

I probably don't need to spend much time convincing you "the days are evil," as Paul wrote. Don't get sucked into the wormhole of endless updates and tweets. Get out and do something that matters. Like many other hobbies that may not actually have a powerful eternal significance, it's obviously fine to spend time on these platforms. Just "be careful how you live" and stay away from the social wormhole. I want my life to matter and spend my time wisely.

Author and artist Paul Jarvis probably explains this best:

> "The less time you spend catching up
> on what you think you're missing out
> on, the more time you can actually
> live your life, do your work, or
> connect with others in a present
> way."

Written

People who lived in biblical times obviously faced unique challenges we do not face today, and the opposite is also true. Most of us don't face the temptation to bow down in worship to wooden idols, but Paul and John never had to deal with distant relatives who seem to "like" and awkwardly comment on everything you ever post on Facebook.

Equal burdens to carry, I'm sure.

Posting on social networks as we know it today wasn't possible back in those days, but the written word was the furthest development of human communication at the time. A good chunk of our New Testament is comprised of letters written by one man to a larger group of people. The letters to the people living in Corinth or Ephesus were intended to be read aloud and passed around for many people to read and discuss. For lack of a better comparison, Paul, John, Peter and the others were "posting" ideas and updates for large audiences to consume. In that sense, their letters were the core of what we now consider "social networking."

Luckily there was no documented poking.

Interestingly, the letters of 2 and 3 John both end with almost identical wording. 2 John 12 reads, "I have much to write to you, but I do not want to use paper and ink. Instead, I hope to visit you and talk with you face to face, so that our joy may be complete."

And again in 3 John 13-14: "I have much to write you, but I do not want to do so with pen and ink. I hope to see you soon, and we will talk face to face." John didn't shy away from sharing thoughts on paper (one man posting a message for many to read), but he also recognized that some conversations are best to have one-on-one, in person, in the same room.

Technology has come such a long way. Skype and FaceTime are awesome tools. Before my wife and I got married, there was a season when I was working in Colorado and she was going to school in Kansas. We only got to see each other once a month or so (if we were lucky). We would text and Skype and Facebook, but it just wasn't the same. We drove for miles and spent hours on I-70 for a chance to spend a day or two together. Sometimes pen and ink—or virtual pen and ink and cell phone cameras—just didn't cut it. As John put it, our "joy was complete" when we were physically in the same room, pixel-free.

Jesus.

Let's look at the example of Jesus once again. In Matthew 13, Jesus' teaching attracted so many people that apparently He literally ran out of land to stand on. In order to make room for the masses, He hopped on a boat by the shore so more people could cram into the space where His voice would carry. We don't know the total number in attendance, but it was obviously a big crowd.

When Jesus spoke to large groups like this, He often spoke in parables. He knew that a lot things He had to say were difficult for human minds to comprehend. He had huge, heavenly principles to share to crowds of people who would have had limited education. More than 2,000 years later, the smartest men and women in human history still struggle to grasp these same concepts. So when He was in front of those crowds, Jesus tried to relate His talks to stuff they would understand, like seeds and bread and farming and family.

In this instance, Jesus shares a parable about a farmer spreading some seeds.

> "A farmer went out to sow his seed. As he was scattering the seed, some fell along the path, and the birds came and ate it up. Some fell on rocky places, where it did not have much soil. It sprang up quickly, because the soil was shallow. But when the sun came up, the plants were scorched, and they withered because they had no root. Other seed fell among thorns, which grew up and choked the plants. Still other seed fell on good soil, where it produced a crop—a hundred, sixty or thirty times what was sown."
> (Matthew 13:3-8)

Later that day, Jesus' disciples came to Him and asked to help them understand. I'm guessing these 12 men probably enjoyed Jesus' cute little story, but wondered if there was something grander they were missing.

The principle I'm getting at is this: Jesus customized His communication strategy depending on the size and makeup of His audience. He spoke broadly and practically for the huge crowds. He went into more detail with His 12 closest friends who He knew more about. He knew what they could and couldn't understand on a deeper and more personal level. Even more specific still, Jesus often withdrew from the 12 and hung out with just Peter, James, and John.

During His time on earth, Jesus had rings of social

circles. He spoke one way to the crowds of three and five thousand. He went into more detail with the 12, but He reserved His most important moments for His small group of 3.

I think we should do the same. Most of us do this already without putting much thought to it. If you get a new job, decide to propose to your girlfriend, or get the news that you're expecting your first child, you probably tell some people face-to-face, some over the phone, and others with a witty and creative Instagram post. Depending on which social ring the people in your life fall on, they receive news from you differently.

How would your mom respond if she found out you were pregnant by reading a post on Facebook? She would probably freak out and be hurt, right? What you're essentially saying to her is that you're valuing your relationship with your mom just as equally as you value the relationship with the friend from high school you had one chemistry class with and haven't spoken with in 10 years.

Or another example: Do you remember the whole "Top eight" thing on MySpace? The idea was you were supposed to chose eight of your closest friends and family on the network, and those people were displayed in a separate and special section of your profile. I swear there was *bloodshed* at my high school over the Top 8. If you took someone out of your Top 8, you were making a drastic statement about friendship and social status!

The early 2000s were such a weird time.

Back to Jesus and His teaching style, I think He sets an

important and wise model for us to follow. For the most important conversations in life—things about marriage, parenting, even faith and salvation—those conversations are likely best to have with your closest friends in face-to-face conversation. More on this in a minute.

Oh Snap.

There are some people that for whatever reason are against social media. Maybe they are concerned about the privacy settings or maybe they think it's a silly fad. Some simply choose not to add one more piece of clutter to their lives, and all of those are legitimate and perfectly reasonable opinions.

One quick side note: this discussion is very much tied to the previous chapter on relevance. Since managing social media accounts has been part of all of my jobs since college, I spend a lot of time researching and experimenting with the latest networks. Because of the nature of my work, it's important for me to know about and be active on new networks that popup.

Can I be honest for a minute? SnapChat makes me feel old. Like 3 billion years old. *I don't get it.* I find the interface to be confusing. It's weird and creepy to me that everything people send to me instantly disappears forever. It looks and feels like a glorified text message to me, and people's "stories" could easily transfer to different just as effectively to other mediums.

If you remember the definition of "relevant" we talked about ("having significant and demonstrable bearing on the matter at hand"), SnapChat isn't relevant for me. It's *current,* but not relevant. I don't have a significant or demonstrable understanding of how to use the tool. I could force myself to be active for a few weeks and snap ridiculous selfies with dumb captions to send to my Ghost friends (see? Not relevant.), but it would feel awkward and forced. People would know I was uncomfortable. I wouldn't be real.

I regularly have older people at my church tell me they aren't on Facebook and don't understand Twitter, and they're half apologizing and half rebelliously standing their ground. Every week at our church, we print out our email newsletter for people who don't have email accounts. I honestly have a lot of respect for those people. The world has changed so much in the past few years. It's easy to feel left behind, even for people like me who work hard to stay up on trends. We shouldn't force or guilt anyone into using any communication tool they're not comfortable with. Be yourself and only do what you're comfortable with.

By the way, you know the Social Circle of Life, don't you? New social networks lose virtually all of their cool points as soon as they're adopted by moms and McDonalds. Think back; it's true. As soon as teens and college kids realize they're being watched by parents and employers and ads for huge corporations start appearing, they're out and on to the next thing. Don't like the latest trend? Wait it out. It's almost dead anyway.

Medium.

Now, whether you like, love, or hate social media, I think it's important to remember the reality that Facebook, Twitter, Pinterest, and the rest are really just communication mediums. Without impressing you with my deep knowledge about communication theory (sarcasm), "mediums" (or, using the grammatically correct plural "media") are simply any tool that can be used to share a message. A piece of paper is a medium you can use to write a message. The air is a medium used to carry the vibrations from our vocal cords that we then decode into words and sentences. Facebook and Twitter, much like email or instant messaging, are mediums we can use to share a message.

There is nothing essentially "good" or "bad" or "holy" or "evil" about any of those mediums. If everything else is equal (the size of your audience, the words you choose, your intentions, etc.), you can do just as much harm with a mean hand-written letter than you can with a mean 140-character tweet. Remember the "Burn Book" in the "Mean Girls" movie? Even simple pieces of paper that get quickly passed around to a lot of people can cause insane amounts of damage. You can also share just as much joy with a vocal compliment than you can with a Facebook like or share.

Mediums—or media—by themselves are not right or wrong; how we *use* them *can* be right or wrong. Although we can share the same message on any medium, there are certain messages that work best on certain media. That's why John used words on a piece of paper to share a lot of messages, but reserved others for when he could share a message face-to-face. Some things are just more appropriate to talk about over a cup of coffee or a nice meal. Some things don't translate well with the written word (although the creation of emojis certainly helps! I can't even tell you how helpful the hamburger icon has been in my texts). There is no substitute for face-to-face human interaction.

This is what causes trouble on social media. It is possible to have a healthy back-and-forth discussion on Twitter, but just because it's possible doesn't mean it's always the best communication tool. In fact, to use Paul's words we discussed earlier, it is often "fruitless."

Location, Location, Location

On social media, you are broadcasting one message to (usually) a large group of people. Social networks are very effective tools for communicating to your outermost and largest ring of social circles. Since most of us won't stand on a boat speaking to thousands of people, this is our easiest and most practical way to address a large group similar to how Jesus did. These tools are *excellent* at sharing news that lots of people care to listen to, whether that be a major milestone in your life, a funny or inspirational quote that adds value to others' lives, photos of your family, things like that.

Continuing with this analogy, the next level of social circles (closer friends and family that you regularly communicate with) deserves a little more information. These people care about details of your life that most people on Facebook don't care about. I talk to my parents about the repairs I had to do on my car. I tell stories about my vacation to my small group from church. I text my brother YouTube links and super hero movie rumors because I know he'll enjoy them as much as I do.

Finally, we get to your innermost circle of closest friends and family. For me, this is basically my wife and occasionally my closest friends. We go deeper in our conversation and there are very few things we don't share. This ring is interesting because these conversations include silly, insignificant details like what I had for lunch, but also include deep and difficult topics like what I really believe about politics and my deepest questions and wrestling about my faith. Most of my friends don't care what kind of burrito I ordered at Taco Bell, and the deep, truly important conversations I have with my wife are very difficult to have with the 1,000 people I'm connected to on Facebook. Do you realize how small 140 characters are? It is definitely possible to share substantive and worthwhile things via Twitter, but the hardest and best and most passionate conversations deserve much more than a handful of words and hashtags.

I don't think anyone has ever changed their mind about faith in Jesus because of someone's inspirational tweet.

I don't think anyone has ever switched political parties because of a silly meme poking fun at Joe Biden.

I don't think anyone has second-guessed their stance on gay marriage because of a hurtful quote or cherry-picked Scripture verse.

If any of the above things have happened to you, please email me. Seriously. I would love it if someone proved me wrong, because it would make life so much easier. It's *much* harder to engage in face to face conversation about religion or politics with someone who holds the opposite stance as you. My heart beats fast and I begin to sweat when I know I have to say something difficult to a friend who I believe is heading down a dangerous path. Sometimes I hear people say things about politicians or religious leaders that I know for a fact are inaccurate, and it's really hard to stand up and respectfully dialogue about touchy subjects. If you're telling me all I have to do is yell my opinions with exclamation marks and all caps online, sheesh—that would make my life so much easier!

The whole theme of this book is that things worth doing are difficult. Life is hard, and usually "the hardest thing and the right thing are the same," to quote the band The Fray. Being "social"—both online and off—is difficult. There are easy ways and difficult ways to talk about things that matter. I'll let you guess which ones are typically more effective.

Want to live upstream? Change how you view social media. They are *great* tools that I love using. But let's be different from the crowd and use them appropriately. Don't waste your life on fruitless deeds, and share your life with loved ones using appropriate mediums. Remember to be very careful how you live—and what you "like."

6 -- RIGHT

Jesus was a brilliant teacher. Whether you believe He is the Messiah or not, Christians and non-Christians alike seem to agree that Jesus was an incredibly wise man who was among the best communicators to ever walk the earth. No other man has impacted human history the way Jesus did.

If you read through Jesus' teaching in the Gospels, you'll see He continually used two main teaching methods to explain deep and difficult truths: telling stories and asking questions. We often talk about and analyze His parables, but I think today's church has forgotten that asking questions was also an important part of Jesus' teaching style.

For one example, after Jesus told the parable of the Good Samaritan in the book of Luke, Jesus looked to His audience and asked them to help wrap up the lesson.

"Which of these three do you think was a neighbor to the man who fell into the hands of robbers?"

The expert in the law replied, "The one who had mercy on him."

Jesus told him, "Go and do likewise." (Luke 10:36-37)

There's something powerful and a little more guilt-inducing when you have to solve the problem yourself, instead of just being told a blanket rule to follow or principle to live by.

My pastor recently shared some numbers that blew my mind. Throughout the Gospels, Jesus was asked 183 questions. He only directly answered three of them. Jesus *asked* 307 questions.

He knew the answers.

Instead of blatantly exclaiming theological statements of truth, Jesus often chose to ask His disciples (and skeptics) questions that led to deeper thought and conversation. The same was true with Paul and other early church leaders who travelled region to region debating and reasoning with people who held alternative worldviews.

This isn't just true with Christian leaders in the Bible. The Greek philosopher Socrates was also famous for asking questions—so much so that you may be familiar with the "Socratic method" of learning where teachers encourage deeper learning by asking their pupils directed questions that lead them to reaching their own conclusions. When you are forced to internally wrestle with multiple potential answers or solutions, critical thinking enhances your understanding.

Troublemakers.

Over the past few years, several prominent Christians have asked some difficult questions. Jars of Clay frontman Dan Haseltine found himself in a heated Twitter battle after asking questions about gay marriage online. Michael Gungor has received all kinds of criticism after asking questions about creation and sharing skepticism about the historical accuracy of Noah's Ark. Venues have cancelled concerts, bookstores have pulled albums from retail, and bloggers have gone wild with hurtful labels and accusations.

Just to keep things civil and G-rated, I won't even go into what people have said about Rob Bell. Google it if you dare. Just make sure your "Safe Search" is turned on.

Christianity is hard. The Bible makes a lot of claims that are difficult to understand, and the biblical writers don't expand as much as we may want them to on issues like hell, creation, the Trinity, sexuality, marijuana, border control, or any other heated issue featured on news networks and online discussion boards. For example, wouldn't life in the 21st century be even a tiny bit easier and clearer if Jesus directly addressed homosexuality? Other biblical writers certainly address the issue, but we have no record of Jesus talking about it. He is also strangely silent about social security, tattoos, and medical marijuana.

Our religious views ultimately come down to faith and interpretation. Jesus never apologized for offering a way of life that would be difficult to understand (remember that whole "narrow road" thing?). He could have made the Scriptures more clear and blatant if He wanted to, but instead God chose to leave a lot of our questions unanswered or even completely unaddressed. The ones who find the full life He promised would have to have faith—not facts and easy explanations.

As frustrating as it can be, there is also something important and comforting about the mystery and incomprehensible wisdom of our God. I wouldn't want to follow a God that was just as smart as I am. I don't want to figure Jesus out completely. As soon we do, there would be no need for faith. As we read in Hebrews, "Now faith is confidence in what we hope for and assurance about what we do not see." (Hebrews 11:1)

Faith, by this definition, can't be absolutely proven. If it could be scientifically verified, we would base our religion on facts. But that's not how God designed this whole thing.

There's a lot we don't know.

In the book of Job, we read that God is "beyond understanding" (Job 36:26). Paul tells the church in Ephesus that God is able to do more than we can ever imagine (Ephesians 3:20). God spoke through the prophet Isaiah to tell us, "My thoughts are not your thoughts, neither are your ways my ways" (Isaiah 55:8).

If there is one thing the Bible *is* clear about, it's that we will never understand everything this side of heaven. We don't have it all figured out, and we never will. So, when people ask questions about issues that are divisive, controversial, and difficult (impossible?) to understand, how should Christians react?

I would venture to say that we haven't handled it very well. This has sadly always been true, but it seems we have only become more bitter and divisive among ourselves in recent years. A lot of responses to Haseltine and Gungor that I've read lately weren't necessarily dripping with love or respect. We are *so* quick to default to criticism and hurtful labels when fellow believers are bold and vulnerable enough to share their internal wrestlings. Especially online, we have helped to create an atmosphere that is very hostile to questions and doubt.

Which scenario would you rather have: prominent Christian leaders like Haseltine and Gungor asking tough and controversial questions, or have them blindly follow cultural norms and constantly push down their doubts and questions, refusing to address the pain and struggles they're having?

Reason.

God created us with brains that are capable of reasoning, grappling, imagining, and conversing. Jesus even instructed us to love God with our *minds* (Luke 10:27).

When Christians talk about faith with unbelievers, we often encourage them to use their minds. We appeal to reason when we ask seekers how such a complex universe could be created randomly and accidentally. We may bring up the common strand of morality that crosses time and culture that must have come from somewhere (why is love always good and hate is always bad? Didn't that have to come from somewhere?). Christians have spent centuries researching and cross-checking historical evidence to prove the validity of Scripture. When talking to outsiders, it is common for believers to ask questions that have rational and thoughtful responses.

If that's the case, why do we get so harsh and angry with other Christians when they ask tough questions? Why is doubt and curiosity so frowned upon in our churches? Why do we allow ourselves to say such hurtful and damaging things about fellow brothers and sisters in Christ? How is our house supposed to stand if we are so divided?

Hint: Jesus said it couldn't (Mark 3:25).

The toughest question of all

I think Jesus would be ok with His people asking tough questions. In fact, in the Scriptures we see that Jesus Himself asked the most controversial question of all time.

> Jesus and His disciples went on to the villages around Caesarea Philippi. On the way He asked them, "Who do people say I am?"
>
> They replied, "Some say John the Baptist; others say Elijah; and still others, one of the prophets."
>
> "But what about you?" He asked. "Who do you say I am?" (Mark 8:27-29)

Now *that's* a good question. Just who is Jesus? Is He the son of God? Is He a good moral teacher? Did He raise from the dead? Does He have the power and authority to die for our sins? Did He ever actually live at all?

Our answer to *those* questions—not our stance on marriage or creation or any other issue—is what our lives ultimately come down to.

Essentials.

One of my favorite quotes of all time comes from St. Augustine. When discussing differences in beliefs, here was his stance:

> "In essentials, unity;
>
> in non-essentials, liberty;
>
> in all things, charity."

This gets messy, of course, because we could (and people have!) spend days, years, or lifetimes arguing whether specific issues are essentials or non-essentials. Stop and really think about this: Do we *have* to agree about our stance on homosexuality in order to be Christians? What about predestination? Do we have to agree on a seven-day creation narrative?

Most dictionaries use words like "indispensable" or "absolutely necessary" to define the word "essential." So, is our stance on marijuana or our beliefs about creation "absolutely necessary" for our salvation? Maybe a harder question: Do you think our faith is "dispensable" (or unnecessary or replaceable) if we have different views on important things like marriage? As important as those things are, is it worth completely disowning people who otherwise love and want to follow Jesus? Are people not going to heaven because they don't believe in Noah's Ark?

To me, those are easy questions. *Of course* we should still love those people. The deeper you get into faith and theology, you're *going* to have differences with people (if nothing else) simply because the Bible does not 100% specifically spell out many of the things we have questions about. If you have a magical fifth Gospel book I'm missing, please let me know (although I may have a few questions about *that*).

There is an interesting exchange in Mark 9 where Jesus addresses this. John told Jesus that he had recently seen some people going around casting out demons in Jesus' name, but John told them to stop "because he was not *one of us*." Here was Jesus' response:

> "Do not stop him," Jesus said. "For no one who does a miracle in my name can in the next moment say anything bad about me, for *whoever is not against us is for us.*" (Mark 9:39-40)

Sadly, I think a lot of Christians are pretty good at stopping people who don't act like "one of us." Jesus' response is really interesting to me. The men who were casting out demons must have been Jesus followers, because they invoked the power of His name, and the demons did in fact leave. I'm not sure what made these men stand out as different to the disciples, but Jesus said it didn't matter; they were on the same team.

If you have someone in your life who claims to follow Jesus and agrees on the essentials, don't chastise them if they look or believe differently than you do. Whoever is not against us is for us.

Charity.

Let's go back to that Augustine quote for a minute. "In essentials, unity; in non-essentials, liberty; in all things, charity." I think we all probably have a decent understanding of the words unity and liberty, but let's look at charity.

Personally, when I hear that word, my mind immediately jumps to donating money. That's what we do with charities, right? If someone is running a 5K for cancer awareness, we give them money. If a horrible natural disaster strikes, we give money to the Red Cross. Maybe you donate money to your church or your school, or maybe you give your clothes to Goodwill.

Those are all good examples of charity, but the word is actually much deeper than those examples. If you look up "charity" in the dictionary, one of the definitions probably includes something like "Christian love; agape."

Now we're just getting into vocabulary inception. Hang with me for a minute and let's see if the top ever stops spinning.

"Agape" is another word you've probably heard before, but let's recap. In the Bible, there are three kinds of love used in the original Greek language: philia (brotherly love, general kindness), eros (sexual, physical love), and agape. Agape is the most difficult to define, probably because it is the most rare kind of love in our culture today.

Agape love is what the Bible says God shows to

humanity. Agape love is deep and powerful and merciful and all-encompassing. "Agape" is the word used over and over again in 1 Corinthians 13 (the love chapter), that tells us that love is patient and kind. Agape love keeps no record of wrong. Agape love is not self-seeking. Agape love endures through every circumstance.

Agape love is deep and powerful and personal. Agape love is forgiving and humble. And *that* love? *That's* what St. Augustine said we're supposed to show to *everyone*. In the context of the quote above, it's what we're supposed to show to people who disagree with us. That is charity.

Or as Jesus put it, we're supposed to "agape" our *enemies* and pray for those who persecute us (Matthew 5:44). So, if you're like John and not sure if someone is on your side or not, we *at least* have to love them unconditionally.

Purpose.

There are a handful of times in Scripture where Jesus or other important authors are asked to summarize the purpose of human existence (no big deal, right?). Carefully read Micah 6:8:

> "What does the Lord require of you?
> To act justly
> and to to love mercy
> and to walk humbly with your God."

In the New Testament, a leader and apparently very religious man asked Jesus what the greatest commandment was.

Jesus replied: "'Love the Lord your
God with all your heart and with all
your soul and with all your mind.'

 This is the first and greatest
commandment. And the second is
like it: 'Love your neighbor as
yourself.' All the Law and the
Prophets hang on these two
commandments."
(Matthew 22:37-40)

According to Jesus, the two most important things we
are supposed to do on this earth are to love God and love
others. And what kind of love are we supposed to show?

You guessed it; *agape*.

In Romans, we're told to live at peace with everyone "if
it is possible, as far as it depends on you" (Romans 12:18). We
are given responsibility to live with a spirit of unity and charity
and agape with anyone who remotely gives you a chance.

If Jesus is ok with questions, I think we should be, too.

Go upstream. When people disagree with you, show
them charity. Love your friends, neighbors, and enemies even
if—no, *especially* if—their opinions differ from yours.

7 -- LOUD

When my dad was first teaching me how to drive, I remember one specific moment when we were about to wrap up a training session. I had recently championed my running-over-the-curb issues and was overall getting the hang of operating a vehicle. On our way home, I remember looking over to my dad with a smirk.

> "Hey dad, you've done a great job at teaching me and everything, but I think there's one thing we haven't gone over yet."
>
> ... "Oh yeah?" says my very thorough engineer father.
>
> "Yes. I need to practice driving with loud music."

You see, whether I'm in the car, at home, the office, or literally anywhere else, I *always* have music playing. I don't do well with silence, and usually my music is loud (just ask the guy whose office is right next to mine).

We all have *that one song*, don't we? That one special track that is always the first thing you play every time you get a new stereo, or the power song on your iPod as you force yourself through a workout? That one song that somehow has an extra punch to your soul? For me—and most Christian kids raised in the 90s—it was always "Meant to Live" by Switchfoot. With a slight roll of the eyes from my loving father, the 16-year-old me cranked up the volume in my baby blue 1987 Honda Civic on our journey home going 40 miles per hour with my hands at 10 and 2.

"Da na na—waaaahahhhh, da na na waahhaaaaa…"

Online

The Internet is both a great and horrible thing. One of the best and worst things about it is that *any*one *any*where can publish *whatever* they want about *any*thing *any*time.

You already see the problem, don't you?

There's a lot of noise.

A few months ago we had a round of local elections to vote on our state's leaders in congress. To be frank, I don't do a terrific job at following the latest news coming out of Washington. Still, when the elections roll around, I want to do my civic duty and be an informed citizen ("Cuz I'm prooouuudd to be an American! Where at least I know I'm freeeeee….").

When I was doing my research about our local candidates, I hate to admit that I eventually gave up. Not surprisingly, the candidates' "official" webpages only had glowing positive things to say, and it was difficult to see where they actually stood on some of the issues. Other websites made bold claims about one candidate's past, and a different article made the complete opposite claim. Of course the local TV ads aren't any help, and bloggers on both sides seem to write whatever will further help their biased cause whether there is any evidence to back up their claims or not. The truth is sometimes incredibly difficult to find in the midst of so much noise.

Politicians are always an easy target, but it's not just happening with presidents and senators.

Recently there was a very controversial call made by a referee in an NFL playoff game. When I started scrolling through Facebook after the game, I (sadly) knew what I was going to find: a lot of noise. People were going *nuts*. Many people were calling for the official's job. Others were claiming conspiracy theories about bribery and corruption. Video replays and grainy screenshots were everywhere, and seemingly everyone had a strong opinion, whether they typically watched football or not. Lots of... "colorful" words were being used quite liberally.

Let's talk about referees for a minute. They, too, are easy targets, and I admit I sometimes get riled up at sporting events when I disagree with a call. I've learned a lot about reffing the past few years from my friend Nathan who refs for high school and college football games in our area. A few months ago he showed me a special resource he has access to where *every single call* the referees made that season were explained. Like, *all* of the actual calls made in the games. A committee watched the game footage and ruled whether they made the correct call or not. A detailed explanation was provided as to why they did or didn't do the right thing. You could click on plays and watch the replays. A vast majority of the time, the referees made the right call—in *real time*. They obviously couldn't pause reality or even watch the replay on every call, but these guys are pros that go to all sorts of meetings and training camps—yes, training camps—to prepare for these games.

All this for high school and college games—in the middle of Kansas.

Do you think NFL referees calling a playoff game might know a little more than you do about pass interference?

Maybe.

Moments like these are when social media is at its worst. I'm honestly embarrassed to be friends with some of the people I scroll through on Facebook when some kind of buzzy news breaks.

And you know what? Christians seem to be the worst. Collectively we have gotten very good at cherry-picking Scripture verses that back our claims, whether our opinions are actually biblical or not.

Don't read this part. You'll just get angry.

I want to choose my next few words very carefully. I may step on some toes (and I've been working out, so it may hurt), but this is something I am passionate about:

Be ruthlessly and tirelessly careful with the noise you make.

A lot of Christians make a lot of really bad noise—and I'm not talking about those silly teenagers with their drums and guitars and rock n' roll music. This noise is much more damaging. I'm frankly ashamed to be associated with Christians sometimes. We collectively say some horrible things. I find myself strangely resonating with the famous quote from Mahatma Gandhi:

> "I like your Christ. I do not like your Christians. Your Christians are so unlike your Christ.

Of course I'm mainly talking about politics and other cultural issues that have become increasingly divisive in recent years. Whether we're talking about homosexuality, abortion, war, border control, marijuana, or just about anything else, I've heard some very uninformed and hurtful comments from Christian friends. It's so easy to default to an us-vs-them, they're-wrong-and-sinful-and-I-have-a-perfect-understanding-of-Scripture knee-jerk reaction. I understand it, and I'm aware that I'm occasionally guilty of it myself.

That reaction—the loud I'm-right-you're-wrong reaction—whichever side you're on with any particular issue—*that's* the wide gate. Most people go that route because it's easy and it's tempting and it somehow feels good. But I believe there's a better way.

America. (Don't read this section either)

As Christians, it's ok (and good!) for us to stand up for things like biblical marriage or whatever topic you're passionate about. It's no secret that the world is a mess. Sin is everywhere. It is sad how much our culture has turned from Christian ideals, and it's even ok to mourn that fact. While that is true, let's also have a quick overview of American history. Are you ready for this?

America is not a Christian country.

Put your pitchforks down and hear me out.

The pilgrims came to America to pursue religious freedom. They came across the pond because they were being persecuted, so they established a new nation where the inhabitants could choose what they believed and how they worshiped. The Constitution clearly states:

> "Congress shall make no law respecting an establishment of religion, or prohibiting the free exercise thereof."

Notice it doesn't say anything about Christianity. So, not only is America not a Christian nation, but it would be *illegal* to pursue that idea. The beauty and difficulty of America is that we are free. We get to choose who we worship—if we worship anything at all.

Let's play this out a little. What if a Muslim was elected president, and suddenly 100% of Congress also mysteriously converted to Islam. It would be illegal for them to force any of their ideals unique to their religion on the rest of the country. Thank goodness, right? We have total freedom of religion, regardless of which particular belief system is the most popular or which one many of our founding fathers claimed.

If freedom and democracy are at the core of our country, and if we want to be law-abiding citizens who submit to governing authorities (like we're instructed to do in Romans 13), we have to be ok with and respect people who have different opinions from us (plus there's always that pesky "love your enemies" thing). That's why America was formed.

With that in mind, it's no wonder so many people hold views that differ or flat out contradict the Bible. That freedom of thought is what makes America, America. Not everyone gets to decide those kinds of things. We are lucky and blessed to live in freedom—and it would be wise for us to recognize that those on the opposite side of the fence from us have that exact same freedom as long as it does not break any other laws.

Sadly, another common theme throughout Scripture is that our views and our decisions will never be popular during our time on earth. If they were easy, I wouldn't be writing this book. In 1 John 3, John writes "Do not be surprised, brothers and sisters, if the world hates you." Peter refers to us as foreigners, exiles, or (in some translations) "aliens" in the world (1 Peter 2:11). We are called to live and think differently, and because of that, everyone else taking the wide path will think we're weird for branching out. We have to be very careful then how we live (Ephesians 5:15).

I admit this is sticky. Part of the reason for our existence as Christians is to try to help spread the word about Jesus. Even if the world is hostile towards our message, our Creator instructed us to tell everyone what we believe. Please don't hear me incorrectly. I'm not saying we should surrender and give up when people challenge our beliefs. Far from it. Here's what I am trying to say:

You will not change someone's mind about homosexuality or abortion or even the deity of Jesus with hate and anger and yelling. You simply will not.

Today—as I type these words—our nation is celebrating Martin Luther King, Jr. Day. I can't help but reflect on his incredible life as I think through these ideas. If there was *anyone* who understood this concept, it was Dr. King. As he so perfectly and eloquently stated:

> "Darkness cannot drive out darkness; only light can do that. Hate cannot drive out hate; only love can do that."

And again:

> "Love is the only force capable of transforming an enemy into a friend."

Your negative and hurtful Facebook post will not change anyone's mind about Jesus. Your passing comment about gay people at a social gathering could have way more emotional damage than you ever realize. Your angry jab at Republicans or Democrats or Independents or Libertarians does no good. You may not be "hateful," but you are putting out a lot of noise.

Noise doesn't change people's minds.

Love is the only force capable of doing that.

(Ok, you can read this now)

After that section, I'm guessing you fit into one of two camps: either you're ticked and you're about to burn this book and demand a refund, or you're cheering me on and screaming "Amen, brother!" and maybe underlining or tweeting something. If you're in the former, I'm sorry I offended you. If you're in the latter, I'm about to offend you.

We all do this.

Maybe it's not always about politics, but humans are stinkin' stubborn. We all think we're right 100% of the time, but that is impossible since we are human. I have to address the awkward elephant in the room that there are almost certainly things in this book that aren't accurate. I admit that I'm probably wrong about some of the things I believe. I'm not wrong on purpose. The things in this book and the things in my mind are simply my best interpretation of Scripture and of the nudging of the Holy Spirit up to this point in my life. I will very likely think differently even in a few years. Right now I'm simply doing the best I can to read my Bible every day, pray for wisdom and discernment, and surround myself with helpful, Godly people. I hope you'll choose to do the same.

Deep breath. Ok. Now that all of that is out of the way, how on earth are we suppose to be "in, not of" the world? How can we passionately stand for what we believe in without inadvertently hurting others with our noise? Let's see what Paul had to say.

Be quiet.

When Paul was writing his letters to the church in Thessalonica around 52 A.D., there were no nationally broadcast football games or democratic elections as we know them today. People definitely weren't publishing their personal opinions about matters like these the way we do today. Still, his words nearly 2,000 years ago seem strangely relevant and applicable to our world today:

"Make it your ambition to lead a quiet
life: You should mind your own
business and work with your hands,
just as we told you, so that your daily
life may win the respect of outsiders
and so that you will not be dependent
on anybody."
(1 Thessalonians 4:11-12)

Out of all of the things I've discussed so far, leading a
quiet life has to be among the most difficult. Quiet is a word
most of us don't like. I admit that I'm probably among the
worst at avoiding silence. Plus, arguing is just so much fun.

As followers of Jesus, one of the primary purposes of
our existence is to share our faith with others. Part of God's
will for our lives is to tell our friends, family, and neighbors
about our Savior. That will often include a verbal exchange,
but not always. As St. Francis of Assisi famously said, "Preach
the gospel. Use words if necessary."

If necessary.

In this passage, Paul says we can win the respect of
outsiders simply by the way we choose to live. He said nothing
about fiery and accusatory rants on Facebook. He said nothing
about protest signs. He said nothing about arguments and
debates about hot button political issues. How do we win the
respect of outsiders—those who may not be on our side yet,
but we're still supposed to agape love anyway?

We win their respect *by being quiet.*

In our world today—probably even more so than during

Paul's time—if you are quiet, mind your own business, and work hard, you will stand out. You'll be weird. That is a sadly unique and unheard of concept today. People will notice that you are different. If you don't have a strong desire to constantly promote your good deeds on Facebook, you will earn the respect of outsiders. If you don't use hurtful language to try to get people to agree with you, your chances of actually making a difference are much, much higher. There is something powerfully attractive about quietly living your own life well.

Of course there are times you have to speak up and stand your ground. God also calls us to be bold in the face of persecution. But here's what I'm getting at: *please* be careful with your noise. Whether online or in person, choose your words carefully. By all means, do your research and be informed. Vote. Stand up for what you believe in. Take advantage of the freedoms this country has fought for for centuries.

However, I *beg* you, let us be the generation that turns the tides on matters like these. Be respectful to everyone. Show kindness and grace and forgiveness. Use a little common sense and remember to always research both sides. Remember that the Bible says that we are Christ's ambassadors. As C.S. Lewis wrote, our name—"Christians"—reminds us that our purpose is to become "little Christs." We represent Jesus. Make it your goal to represent Him well so that quote from Ghandi ("Your Christians are so unlike your Christ") is not longer accurate. We *need* to look more like our Christ.

Let's go upstream. Instead of being loud, let's lead a quiet life so we may win the respect of outsiders.

8 -- LEADER

If you've been to a high school or college graduation ceremony recently, you and I have likely heard several similar speeches presented by principals, valedictorians, and special guests. As hard as they may try to avoid this, let's face it; every one of those speeches is the same.

> "Congratulations, graduates! The last four years—or five or six, for those of you on the extended learning plan (snicker)—you have worked hard. You've had to make sacrifices that led you to where you are today. And while we applaud your hard work, we can't forget to honor and thank your parents, friends, and those who love you who have helped you get this far. And while this marks the end of one chapter of your life, it's actually just the beginning. Today you embark on a new journey full of new experiences and new

challenges, and you'll be forced to look back on your years here and lean on the knowledge you've gained to be a successful member of society. But *you,* the class of (fill in the blank), we expect great things from you. You're the future. Now we release you, and we leave you with this charge: Use what you've learned here to make a difference. Be a leader. Be creative. Work hard, and you—yes you!—can change the world!"

...amiright? Queue "Friends Are Friends Forever" with a baby photo montage and give your mom some Kleenex.

In our culture today, we *love* the idea of leadership. We tell everyone to be a leader. We instruct everyone to be creative problem solvers. No matter what their career field might be or what kind of personality they have, we tell all of our students and young adults to strive toward leading or starting something that will *change the world.*

INFJ

I started thinking about this recently when everyone on our church staff took a very detailed personality test. You've probably taken quizzes like this before where you end up with some sort of acronym, symbol, animal, or number that categorizes you as a certain type of individual. The idea is that once you understand your specific combination of characteristics, you can work with your peers more effectively and manage your time more efficiently.

The results of this particular quiz were disturbingly accurate for me. Like usual, there were certain statements that made me feel a sense of pride (like my ability to organize and accomplish tasks), and others that left me with hints of embarrassment and shame (like my desire to please others and my desperate need for approval).

While I found it interesting, this was nothing I hadn't heard before. But towards the end of my automated report, I read two things I didn't expect to see: According to this test, I am not creative and I am not a good leader.

For some strange reason I can't explain, I was crushed about this. Those two statements computed by a robot somewhere hit me really hard. Over the past several years, those were two of the first words I would have used to describe myself. I have quite a bit of leadership experience and my career field requires me to create several new projects every day. And I mean, those graduation speeches! My high school principal and college president told me I was special!

As silly as it sounds, I began to question my identity. Was I wrongfully over-confident in my leadership? Maybe I confused "creativity" with the skill of successfully mimicking other people's ideas. Maybe I was given leadership roles just because I went to a small school. Maybe my view of myself was skewed by a supportive community coaching me to believe I was good at something I really wasn't. If I couldn't lead and I wasn't creative, maybe I needed to completely re-think my career path. Maybe I wasn't really who I thought I was. And even scarier, maybe everyone around me already knew it.

… All of this *from a standardized personality quiz*. Maybe that says something about my personality right there. Yikes.

It may sound ridiculous to you, but I think we all do this

to some extent. Regardless of any amount of success we may have experienced in the past, one small setback can trigger all kinds of doubt in our human minds. We're fragile creatures that can easily be convinced that we're not as special as we thought we were.

One reason those statements hurt me so deeply was because our culture validates and applauds creative leaders. The "normal" everyday people with mid-level, non-glamorous jobs, or those who are great at being second-in-command, or those who are skilled at tasks that are labeled as more mundane? No one celebrates those people. Even if they are hard workers who are great parents and very successful in their roles, those people—who make up a vast majority of the population—are rarely celebrated or recognized.

Going back to those graduation speeches, have you actually thought about the implications of those leadership sentiments? What if *every one* of those students were leaders as we typically define them? Every year *millions* of students graduate high school and college in America. If *each* of them changed the world? My goodness. Talk about turbulence. And probably a lot of horrible ideas. Frankly, I don't want most of my classmates to change the world.

In reality, only a select few people in each generation actually change the world. The rest of us work hard and do our best to lead our families and ourselves well, but that is pretty much the extent of our influence.

And we need to stop thinking of that as a bad thing. Not everyone is a leader. Not everyone is creative. And those are *good things*. We need to value variety, balance, and individuality. We need to embrace the gifts and personality differences God has wired within us.

The world values status. Upstreamers value equality and authenticity.

Family farm.

One of the most beautiful things about our modern structure of living is that it requires us to rely on each other. Gone are the days of the family farm where mom, dad, and the kids are responsible for everything from hunting to making clothes to educating the children and cooking the food. Personally, I'm thankful that I don't have to know how to best utilize every inch of a buffalo to ensure my family's survival. My experience on the Oregon Trail computer game tells me that I likely wouldn't live very long on the open frontier before dying of dysentery. (Can I get an amen?)

As a segmented society, we *need* people with diverse skill sets. I am good at some things, and horrible at others. I need other people in my life who are good at plumbing and building furniture and repairing cars and crunching numbers in Excel. And those people may need other people who are good at designing posters and web pages and making a good cup of coffee. Since we no longer *have* to do everything in order to survive, we're able to become more specialized, which in turn advances our crafts to new heights that were impossible in the past.

If everyone was equally creative and everyone had the exact same set of skills, we wouldn't get very much done and our culture would never advance. We'd still live in little houses on the prairie wearing bonnets and overalls. I, for one, am grateful we've moved past those days. I don't look very good in a bonnet.

Bod.

Paul addresses this issue in 1 Corinthians 12. In his discussion of spiritual gifts, Paul compares the collection of believers around the world to a human body. He points out that although we collectively have a wide variety of talents and experiences, we are called to be *one* body. Our bodies work best and maximize their potential when every part is working properly. Of course we probably all know people who are blind, deaf, crippled, or have some other form of disability who still lead happy and successful lives, but life is generally easier and fuller when each body part does its job as well as it was designed to operate.

In his example, Paul points out how silly it would be if certain body parts tried to rebel.

> Now if the foot should say, "Because
> I am not a hand, I do not belong to
> the body," it would not for that
> reason stop being part of the body.
> And if the ear should say, "Because I
> am not an eye, I do not belong to the
> body," it would not for that reason
> stop being part of the body. If the
> whole body were an eye, where would
> the sense of hearing be? If the whole
> body were an ear, where would the
> sense of smell be?
> (1 Corinthians 12:15-17)

Obviously this is a ridiculous thought and an even stranger mental image (just a huge five-foot ear hanging out, doing nothing but listening...), but Paul's point is clear: "God has placed the parts in the body, every one of them, just as He wanted them to be... As it is, there are many parts, but one body." (1 Corinthians 12:18, 20)

I have to admit that I struggle with jealousy and insecurity. I think we all do. Sometimes I see co-workers who lead their teams so much better than I do and I just *wish* I could lead a meeting and think as strategically as they do.

Sometimes I see my friends who are brilliant video producers and photographers who execute excellent creativity in their storytelling. Do you know people like that who are experts in the same field you're in? It's inspiring, but it also forces you to face your own short-comings. And it doesn't feel very good.

Other friends of mine may not necessarily be super successful in their careers, but they just know how to live a good life. They're always full of joy and are a ton of fun to be around. When they enter a room, somehow everything just feels brighter and less heavy.

Some of my friends know how to dress well. They always look good. Most of them have way more money than I'll ever have and they always have the coolest tech gadgets. Do you know people like that?

It's so easy to look at other people's strengths and measure them against our weaknesses. As insecure as I am about the things I lack, I am also occasionally reminded that sometimes I'm on the *other* side of this insecurity matchup.

Some people look at *my* life and think I'm successful. Some people look at my strengths and wish they could do the things I do well.

On one hand, that thought is flattering and encouraging. But on the other? It makes me sick! I'm a *mess*. I'm *not* a success story. There are a few things I'm good at and God continues to bless me with great experiences, but my goodness; don't model your life after mine! You don't want it! It's *so hard* for me to see the good qualities in myself that others may want to replicate. I'm too busy lusting after the good things *they* have.

The same is true for you. Admit it; you compare yourself to others. Accept it; someone else is comparing themselves to you.

You and *your* life look good and effortless and appealing to them, because we are all different. We all have different strengths, and we all need each other for society to continue to advance and thrive.

Why do churches have just one senior pastor? What if we all tried to hop on stage and start speaking on a Sunday morning? I'm guessing there are a handful of people at your church that you don't want leading the direction of the church. But aside from that, another side effect of having too many people talking is that suddenly no one is listening.

The senior pastor's job may seem more glamorous than the sound guy or the custodian or the nursery worker, but each position is necessary for the church—or business or family or relationship—to be successful. If we all had the same gifts and we all had the same role, our worlds would be boring and would never advance.

I'm talking about *everyone*.

Every business has some sort of organization chart so people know where they stand and who they report to. If we're honest, we all know that the people who are near the bottom of those lists are some of the most critical to a business's success. They may not have very much hierarchical leadership, but they are often invaluable in the company's pursuit of success.

When I was in high school, I quickly learned an important lesson: If you wanted to really get things done (and occasionally get out of trouble), there are three groups of people that you want on your side: custodians, lunch ladies, and secretaries. I can't tell you how many times I got a custodian to unlock a door or even let me in someone's locker when they didn't *really* have permission to do so. One secretary made probably hundreds of copies for me on the school copier that I probably should have paid for. I don't know of any foul play for sure, but occasionally I would hear the lunch ladies talk about students who were mean and disrespectful toward them, and I'm just a firm believer in not biting the hand that feeds you—literally. Those lunch ladies have more power than you realize.

In my world today, my administrative assistant Stacy is one of the most talented people I know. She may not get very much public praise and most people at our church couldn't tell you her name, but she is the secret weapon that keeps our department running. On our org chart, Stacy may not look like an eye or an arm or whatever body part sounds important to you, but she absolutely is necessary for our team to be successful.

I think Paul understood this:

> "Those parts of the body that seem to be
> weaker are *indispensable*, and the parts that we
> think are less honorable we treat with special
> honor. And the parts that are unpresentable
> are treated with special modesty."
> (1 Corinthians 12:22-23)

Let's face it. It is terribly inconvenient to get a broken arm or ear infection, but I thank the good Lord that my anus and urinary tracts are working properly. That's what Paul is talking about, right? The "parts that are unpresentable"? We want those to be functioning. I'd be willing to suffer most injuries and endure most sicknesses before volunteering to pass a kidney stone. In our bodies and in our businesses, *every* part is valuable, and often the unglamorous ones are the most critical to success.

We need each other to buy our stuff.

Artists need successful business people to fund and commission their work. Car mechanics need designers who build their websites and secretaries who answer their phones. Teachers need factory workers who manufacture crayons and magic markers. Police officers need donut shops to give them fuel to chase down the bad guys.

(sarcasm)

When I was in college, I had the amazing privilege of going on mission trips around the world to spread the word about Jesus. You know why I got to go? Of course I believe that those trips fit within God's will for my life, and He orchestrated the situations that led me to those villages in Kenya and those clinics in Egypt. But on a more practical level, I got to go on those trips and tell people about Jesus because our church has several successful and generous families. As a 19 year old studying ministry and art, I didn't have $2,000 to get me to the other side of the world. I couldn't get to China by myself, and most people in my congregation couldn't take off time from work and family to go to the other side of the world.

In order for a good deed to occur, we needed each other to each play our part. Some roles are more glamorous than others to the rest of the world, but one cannot happen without the other.

Spectacles.

Recently I was forced to embrace my mortality and get my first pair of glasses. I've always had great vision and never had trouble reading or seeing the white board in school. I can still see well, but I was starting to realize that after long days at work, my eyes just... hurt. I felt strained and extra tired. At first I blamed it on caffeine or maybe not enough sleep, but as it continued, I began to wonder if it was something deeper.

My doctor explained to me that I have a condition where—after hours of focusing on objects up close—my eyes have a tendency to drift apart. I don't literally go cross-eyed, but my brain has to constantly fight my natural leaning to keep focused on what's in front of me. That constant fight led to strain and fatigue that built over time.

Now that I have glasses, I don't necessarily see *better*. The crispness of objects in front of me doesn't really change. However, with them on, I do see *easier*. With a little help, my eyes are able to do what they were created to do with less stress and less pressure on my body.

Sometimes you can get by leading or not leading or being creative or not being creative even if it isn't how you were naturally built. Humans are good fakers. We can make everyone—including ourselves—believe that we're better at our jobs than we really are. It is possible to fight against your nature and force yourself into a role or position that doesn't fit with your initial leaning just to fit in to a crowd or make yourself look good. But after a while, you'll feel strain. You'll get headaches. You'll get the sense that things should be easier than they are. Your body and your mind will be tired.

Don't strain trying to do something you weren't created to do. Use the tools God has given you to stay focused on what's in front of you. Your family, your friends, your co-workers, and the *world* need you to be you. *That's* how you can change the world; stop trying to change yourself and instead change the world around you by doing what you were made to do.

If you're a leader, lead well and remember to honor, respect, and serve the people under you. If you're not a leader (or you're not "pretty" or rich or strong or funny), don't waste your energy wishing you were something else. As upstreamers, we need to stop idolizing everybody else. We need to stop wishing we were more creative or better with numbers. It's not easy, but it is the best way to live. Being well-rounded is a great goal, but we also need to be humble enough to remember that we can't do it all.

Thank God for your strengths, and thank God for your weaknesses. We need each other, and that's not a bad thing.

CONCLUSION

One of the only things I remember from my college philosophy class is the idea of the "golden mean." This basic idea was originally developed by Aristotle, but has since been adopted and tweaked by several of the world's important thinkers such as Buddha, Confucius, and even Thomas Aquinas (at least according to Wikipedia).

The basic principle is that in most moral decisions or actions, there are two extremes. The classic example is the virtue of courage. On one extreme of the spectrum, an excess of courage may lead to recklessness, causing you to constantly pick unnecessary fights. On the other end, a complete lack of courage would be described as being a coward, always running away from any hint of conflict. The ideal goal that we should strive for is the golden mean in the middle of these two extremes, leading us to a healthy level of courage.

Throughout this book, I hope you hear my heart that

there is nothing wrong with being big, busy, social, etc. These are difficult and complex issues that don't lend themselves to an easy answer or absolutely perfect solution. When facing decisions and actions like the ones discussed here, we should be aiming toward a healthy golden mean. Don't act with reckless abandon on either end of the spectrum, but remember to keep a healthy balance and live with prayerful intentionality.

So now, I'd like to wrap up our time together the same way Peter wrapped up his second letter in the New Testament:

> "You already know these things, dear friends.
> So be on guard; then you will not be carried
> away by the errors of these wicked people and
> lose your own secure footing."
> (2 Peter 3:17)

I hope I've challenged and encouraged you in some way, but I also recognize the fact that most of you probably already knew these things. You're smart people. If you have the Holy Spirit inside of you, I believe He guides your decisions and clears your paths for you according to His will. Sometimes we just need a reminder of what we already know. So be reminded, and don't lose your secure footing.

The journey we're all on isn't an easy one. When life feels heavy and messy, that's probably a good sign. Sometimes God simply allows us to go through trials, but also remember that our goal is the narrow path that very few people choose. The road ahead is rocky and full of thorns, but it comes with a promise: "perissos" life. Life that is full, vehement, powerful, passionate, and all-encompassing.

UPSTREAM

ABOUT THE AUTHOR

Matt Ehresman makes stuff for fun and for a living.
He spends his days designing, filming, writing, and
creating at First MB Church in Wichita, Kansas. His
writing has been published by RELEVANT, Focus on
the Family, Sunday, Converge, and several other
publications. He loves Tillie (his wife), Mountain Dew,
Marvel, and Panera.
Connect with him at mattehresman.com.